The Hidden Facts Of Fashion

FASHIONARY

ISBN 978-988-77110-8-7
SN HFV122304PBCB
Designed and published in Hong Kong
by Fashionary International Ltd
Printed in China

If you have any feedback of the book,
please don't hesitate to send it to
feedback@fashionary.org

@ fashionary
@ fashionary
@ fashionary

Fashionary Team

The Hidden Facts Of Fashion

FASHIONARY

INTRODUCTION

Every piece of clothing has a story.

While most people spend time staying up to speed with the latest fashion trends and runway shows, not everyone will pay attention to the background of the clothing we wear daily.

If you are curious enough to learn about the pieces in your wardrobe, you will find that each garment, even a simple T-shirt, has a story behind it. The Hidden Facts of Fashion shares those stories — from the origin of a piece of clothing, the unique culture it represents, fun little titbits, urban myths, and more.

By revealing little known facts and fascinating stories, you will discover that small details hidden in your garment, right down to a button or the choice of color, was once specially designed for specific reasons. You'll also uncover fashion industry phenomena and helpful hacks.

We hope this book will give you a deeper understanding of the fashion industry, allow you to look at your closet from a new perspective, and — last but not least — be fun to read.

Facts about Industry

Facts about Color

CONTENT

Facts about Outer

Facts about Top

Facts about Bottom

Facts about Intimate

Fashion Hacks

FACTS ABOUT INDUSTRY

Size 8
1950

Size 8
2050

Size 8 in 1950 is much smaller than today's size 8

The question "what size are you?" is often a tricky one. We all know that different brands and manufacturers have different standards – but did you know sizes also varied in history?

You might be wearing a size 0 now, but back in the 1950s someone with the exact same measurements as you might have been wearing a size 8.

Let's take iconic model Twiggy as an example.

During the peak of her fame in the 1960s, she was 5'6" tall, weighed 112 lbs and was a size 8. In today's size standards, she would be wearing a size 00!

But why?

This shift in sizing is a fashion industry hack called "vanity sizing" – a clever way to flatter women's egos, make them feel slimmer, more confident, and that as a result, spend more money shopping for clothes.

The better the economy, the shorter the skirt?

Women's hemlines rise along with stock prices.

While it would be an obvious assumption that the hemline of a skirt or dress would be determined by fashion trends or social status, believe it or not, the economy is another factor that influences how short your skirt is.

The hemline index

This surprising theory presented by George Tailor in 1926 is called the Hemline Index, which suggests that the hemlines of women's clothing fluctuates with stock prices or gross domestic product.

To put it simply, in a financial crisis, there's less money to spend and people buy only what they need – such as practical office wear which is usually knee-length or longer.

However in an economic boom, there's more money to splurge on short skirts or fun dresses in celebration of happier times.

Here are the economic ups and downs and the corresponding hemline length of the time:

1920s	↗	Roaring 20s	above-the-knee flapper dresses
1930s	↘	The Great Depression	mid-calf and floor-length dresses and skirts
1940s	↗	World War II	knee-length "new look" dresses and skirts
1950-60s	↗	Golden Age of Capitalism	knee-length full skirt and miniskirts
1970s	↘	The Great Inflation	midi and maxi skirts
1980s	↗	Reaganomics	miniskirts and ra-ra skirt
1990s	↗	Economic Boom	miniskirts

It is worth mentioning that the economic cycle leads the hemline length by 3-4 years ahead, meaning the hemline does not respond to the stock market immediately, because it takes time for the hemlines to decrease.

A model wears a creation by Mark Fast during his Autumn/Winter 2011 collection show at London Fashion Week February 21, 2011.

So how did skinny become "fashionable"?

The trend of being thin started in the swinging 1960s when iconic British model Twiggy rose to fame. Her trademark boyish cropped hair, long lashes, and super skinny frame became the benchmark for mod beauty.

Unfortunately Twiggy's slender body type was unrealistic for other women who were not naturally slim. This led to extreme dieting and eating disorders as women tried to replicate her look. A new unhealthy obsession started – being thin was in.

The skinny trend lasted for some years, but died out when the "slim-yet-toned" body figure became the new beauty standard during the 1970s and 1980s.

In the mid-1990s, a newly discovered model called Kate Moss was cast in Calvin Klein's underwear campaign, skyrocketing her into superstardom.

Her emaciated frame, dark under-eye circles and pale skin became widely popular as a new beauty ideal - one that glamorized drug addiction, termed "heroin chic".

Women starved themselves to greater extremes to replicate this look, and eating disorders and anorexia were on the rise.

Today, thankfully, the extremes of the 1990s have once again started to fade. While "heroin chic" has given way to a healthier image, the idea that being skinny is fashionable is still prevalent in many parts of society.

The ridiculous pay gap between female and male models

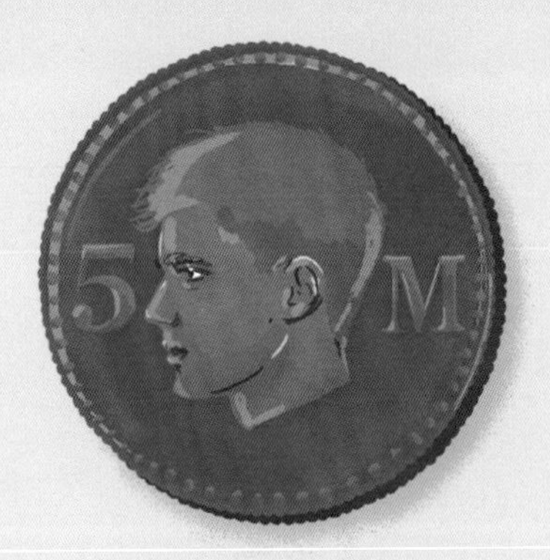

In 2016, the world's number one ranking female model was earning $30 million a year, while the world's top male top model was making $5 million a year.

Existing for centuries, gender inequality is a persistent issue, with women most commonly fighting oppression. You might be surprised to hear that in the modeling industry things are quite the opposite.

In fact, male models are paid a lot less than their female counterparts, even if they are hired for the exact same job.

Let's look at the two top male and female models of 2016, as an example: David Gandy earned $5 million and Gisele Bundchen earned $30 million in the same year.

It's not just the major high-earning models that have discrepancies. Elizabeth Rose, the men's director of premier model management, was quoted recounting a day where a male model was offered $1,900, and a female model $6,300, for the same job.

Why is there such a huge difference between male and female models earning power?

Ultimately it may boil down to sales. Advertisers make more money selling to women who spend more money on female products and therefore are more willing to invest in talent. The opportunity for men to reach supermodel status is greatly reduced when the advertising budget is not available.

But that does not mean female models have an easier career path than males. In fact, the industry treats females pretty harshly by expecting them to start their career at a very young age (usually 14, and peak at 18) and stay young.

Meanwhile, the career path of male models are much longer, as looking youthful is not very important for male models. Mature and even aged male models still have many chances to reach success.

Lipstick vs. Haute Couture: Which makes more money?

Who would have known, a lipstick actually makes more profit than a Haute Couture gown.

Thinking of getting into the haute couture business to profit from luxurious, high-end clothing? You might want to think about getting into the beauty business instead.

While haute couture dresses are perceived as the most desirable and exquisite in the industry – with prices starting at $30,000 and moving up towards $100,000 – they aren't quite as profitable as you might think.

Why?

Well, the labor and time costs related to creating haute couture pieces are incredibly high, and the demand for the creations is low.

Beauty products, on the other hand, can create a high revenue stream because the manufacturing cost is low, while the volume of sales is often high due to the huge market and demand.

Let's look at the facts:

The demand is low
Only 2,000 women worldwide purchase haute couture pieces, and just 200 of those women are regular buyers.

All laborers are specialists
Not just ordinary sewing workings, seamstresses and artisans are all specialty experts, making on average $75,000 a year.

Time cost is high
It's a lengthy process. Haute couture pieces are all handmade and require multiple fitting, it takes approximately 600-1000 hours to make one embellished evening gown.

Exclusive services
Each client has their own personal salesperson, who supervises fittings and ensures the garment design will be exclusive to them. The brands even fly their tailors and sales staff overseas just to fit their clients.

So, what's the point of haute couture?

Think of it as a long-term marketing investment. Often seen on the world's most glamorous women and red carpets, haute couture designs have the ability to boost the image of a brand and in turn create more sales of lower price-point items.

Shopping in outlet stores doesn't always equal a better deal.

Do you really get a better deal in luxury brand outlets?

Outlet stores are a dream for bargain hunters. You can find last season's most-wanted handbag or that pair of shoes you couldn't afford when they were at full price. It sounds like a great deal, right? While it can be, often it really is too good to be true.

Sometimes, not all products in every outlet store are excess products from the main production run, instead, many of them are produced by another manufacturer and assembly line.

These products are often not even found in the original retail stores, and are very likely to be made at a lower cost and quality with adjustments such as subpar material and inferior stitching.

It's speculated that when some of the brands didn't have enough products from the main production run to display in outlet stores, it creates these "outlet-only" items to ensure that the store looks full, and that consumers feel inspired to buy.

Now you know this industry's secret marketing strategy, next time you step foot into an outlet store, it might be best to consider the quality of items more carefully.

Clearance racks are always in a mess for a reason.

Don't be fooled by that messy clearance rack

That messy clearance rack in the corner of the shop may not be due to bad shopkeeping, but instead be designed to look that way. Why would stores create clutter on purpose?

Retailers know that customers prefer to browse a tidy display for ease of finding items – it's all part of an enjoyable retail experience.

The chaotic disarray of the clearance area aims to push you away from products on sale, tempting the eye towards the joyful process of browsing a well-represented rack with regular pricing.

On top of this, even if you do have the patience to tackle the sale items, you're unlikely to change your mind after all the time and effort you spent on finding such a great deal.

So next time you brush past the messy sale rack, why not take a second look? You might be pleasantly surprised.

Alicia Vikander as Caroline Matilda of Great Britain in *A Royal Affair* (2012).

Gugu Mbatha-Raw as Dido Elizabeth Belle in *Belle* (2013).

Different movie, same wardrobe?

Ever wonder what happens to all the costumes after a movie finishes, and how producers deal with sourcing costumes for scenes with large crowds?

Highly recognizable main characters will have costumes preserved or even taken to auction to be sold, and as for crowd actors, most of the clothing is actually shared with other movies.

Big studios often have their own rental houses, allowing smaller producers or studios to rent clothing from them. This also means that it's not unusual to have one costume appear in two different movies. For example, actor Dawn McHargue wore the same costume in Insurgent and Pirates of the Caribbean.

Small studios which have purchased costumes will often host flash sales to get rid of clothing cheaply and quickly.

Through this system of renting, selling and auctioning wardrobes, producers can save money and time purchasing clothing and trying to make it look worn – valuable when you're dealing with the complexities and costs of filming.

RETRO

VINTAGE

ANTIQUE

Vintage, Antique, Retro: What is the difference?

We can thank the hippies during the swinging 1960s for the revolution of vintage clothing. The peace, love and eco-friendly lifestyle of this alternative community changed the mindset towards second-hand clothing and thrift stores.

<u>Vintage</u>
Clothes produced from the 1920s until 20 years ago from today.

<u>Antique</u>
Clothes produced prior to the 1920s.

<u>Retro</u>
Instead of referring to the period clothes are produced, retro refers to clothes that purposely imitate styles from past eras.

For example, if your grandfather passed down a bomber jacket he wore during WW2, that is a vintage bomber jacket. If you bought the latest season's bomber jacket that is designed in a WW2 style, then it is a retro bomber jacket.

<u>The history of second-hand clothing</u>
The business of second-hand clothing has always existed. In the past, only rich people could afford new clothes. Second-hand clothing was a sign of being poor and was undesirable.

During WW2, as lost or abandoned clothing from soldiers ended up in thrift stores, hippies embraced second-hand clothing, as they embraced the values of peace, love and sustainability. Second-hand clothing then started to become fashionable.

Did you know?
The term "vintage clothing" first appeared in 1957 when it was used to describe a pre-loved raccoon fur coat from the 1920s. Before this, pre-loved clothing was referred to as "second-hand" and used merely for practical purposes.

A Swedish power plant burns discarded H&M clothes to generate power.

Don’t throw your clothes into the landfill, turn them into power!

When we no longer wear clothing we own at home, we may take it to a second-hand shop or give it to charity. What do large retail stores that deal with huge volumes of excess or unwearable products do?

There is more pressure than ever before for brands to find sustainable fashion solutions, rather than dump or destroy old products and, in turn, fill up landfills and increase fossil fuel production.

In 2017, it was reported that a Swedish powerplant partnered with fashion retailer H&M to take over and burn the discarded clothing from H&M’s warehouse along with other trash to generate power.

Burning clothing, rather than dumping in a landfill where it cannot be recycled, eases environmental strain as less fossil fuel is burnt. Until 2017, 15 tons of clothing from H&M was burnt alongside other trash.

According to H&M, the discarded clothes does not comply with the restriction on chemicals, rather than simple dead stock.

While the amount may be a small gesture in the scheme of the larger issue, this method might lead to a more environmentally-friendly solution for the fashion industry in the future.

Royal Trend Setter

Without doubt, members of the royal family have always been fashion leaders.

Throughout history, the royal family has been a source of fascination and influence - with the obsession not stopping at just how they live their lives, but the way they choose to dress, too.

Let's take a look at some notable members of the monarchy who not only popularized trends but also redefined lasting traditions in fashion:

Louis XIV, France (1638-1715)

The tradition of fashion season
This was the King who mandated that new textiles and accessories be designed and launched bi-annually. He ruled that visiting nobles should only arrive wearing the latest fashion.
The idea was to stimulate France's economy using the clothing and textile industry. Prior to that, high-fashion was relatively unchanging, and black was the dominant color for clothing.
(For more details, go to page.40)

Queen Victoria, Britain (1819-1901)

Wedding dress codes
Queen Victoria started the tradition of wearing a white wedding dress, and creating the rule that guests should not wear white or long trains.
(For more details, go to page.50)

Black as formalwear
Although the Queen's influence was not the only reason black became fashionable, her choice of wearing black throughout her life to mourn her husband inspired many to do the same.
(For more details, go to page.52)

King Edward VII, Britain (1841-1910)

Children's sailor uniforms
At just four years old, the future king wore a scaled down version of a sailor uniform during a cruise off the channel islands, making it an on-trend choice for children's clothing, and even influenced the uniforms of Japanese school girls.

Cuffed pants and travelers' creases
It's believed that the King's pants were once ironed by a farmer who accidentally put the crease at the front of the garment, rather than the side. Then, to avoid the mud, the King cuffed his trousers to walk outside. Spotted by the media, the look became another trend.
(For more details, go to page.134)

Last suit button left undone
As the King had a rather round body shape, he left the last button of his waistcoat and suit jacket undone for comfort. Out of respect, people followed his example and it soon became the common practice when wearing a suit.
(For more details, go to page.84)

King Charles II, Britain (1630-1685)

Setting the standard of men's formalwear
While King Charles II was not the first man to wear a three-piece suit, he did turn it into the official formalwear for men. The King ordered that the long coat, waistcoat, cravat, breeches, and wigs must be worn in the court. Though the look is not exactly the same today, it was the predecessor of the modern three-piece suit.

Napoleon I, France (1769-1821)

Brass buttons on coat cuffs
It was said that Napoleon was sick of his soldiers wiping their nose and mouth on their sleeves, so he had their uniforms sewn with brass buttons (without any openings or matching buttonholes) to make wiping difficult!

Princess Diana, Britain (1961-1997)

The "revenge" dress
After Prince Charles went public with his affair with Camilla the Duchess of Cornwall, Princess Diana dazzled with a black off-shoulder, cleavage-baring mini dress.

The press named it a "revenge" dress as Diana's actions were seen as a statement to look perfect and confident in the face of betrayal.

The term stuck and today it is still to describe when a woman wants to look her best when dealing with the ending of a difficult relationship.

Why do menswear and womenswear have the opposite front opening direction?

Buttons on the Left

Buttons on the Right

Have you ever noticed that men and women's garments open from different directions?

Take a look at a men's shirt and you'll likely notice that the buttons are on the right, but on a woman's blouse, they are on the left.

It is easy to understand to have buttons on the right side, as the majority of the population are right-handed, this design is easier for the wearer to fasten. But why buttons on women's wear are in opposite side?

One theory is that when buttons started to be used as fastenings in the 13th century, upper-class women were not dressing themselves. Rather, their clothing was fastened by maids and placed on the left-hand side for their convenience.

Now you might think: What about lower class women who do not have maids? Don't tailors take care of their needs?

The truth is, before the industrial revolution, buttons were expensive, ordinary people did not have the luxury to use them.

But no matter whether the theory is true or not, this is a tradition that's stood the test of time, shifting into the 21st century.

It was a constant occurrence that the upper-class would set the trends, and the lower-class would try to emulate their styles as much as possible, but cost often got in the way.

Did you know?
In Eastern traditional costume, front opening direction has a very different background and meaning.

The correct way of wearing Hanfu and Kimono

For Chinese Hanfu and Japanese Kimono, the collar should always been wrapped from the left side over the right, the opposite direction is a way of dressing a dead person.

The way of dead people's wearing

The King who made Paris a fashion capital

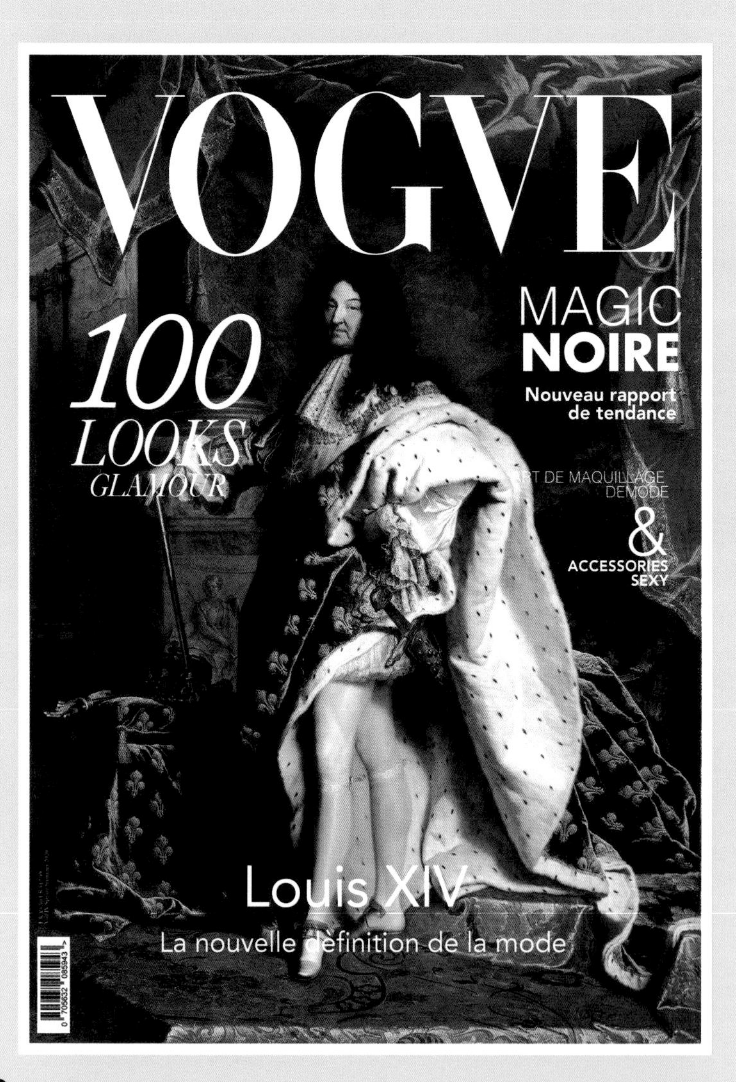

The fashion industry today is dictated by multiple factors. Can you imagine if only one person controlled the entire industry?

The famous French monarch, Louis XIV, used his power and influence to control when and how the fashion and textile industry would operate, and established the standard fashion season as Spring/Summer and Fall/Winter.

It wasn't just for the love of fashion, it was also a business move.

Louis XIV and his finance minister Jean-Baptiste Colbert saw how they could stimulate the economy through the textile industry. They ordered that new fashion, textiles, and accessories be designed twice a year in summer and winter.

He also ordered people visiting the Palace of Versailles to adhere to a dress code: wear the most current trends, head-to-toe.

What's more, he cleverly targeted the upper class knowing that they would have more money to spend on clothing and introduced seasonal trends and fashion plates – all which helped further generate interest in France's booming fashion industry.

Obviously the business plan worked, with Paris becoming the fashion capital of the world, as it is today.

Did you know?
Prior to Louis XIV, the major fashion trend amongst the upper class in Europe was "Spanish style" which meant wearing exclusively black clothing with very little variation, only making occasional allowances for the weather.

FACTS ABOUT COLOR

Blue for girls and pink for boys

Pink for girls and blue for boys. This might be the gender stereotyping of today, but it wasn't always the way.

In the late 19th century to early 20th century, different manufacturers and retailers of baby products have their own claim on the "right" color for boys and girls. Some say pink is for boys and blue is for girls, and some say the opposite.

There were many manufacturers and retailers promoted that red is a color of power and masculinity, and pink was viewed as a "boyish" version of red, while blue is the hue of Virgin Mary's garment.

So if you wanted your boy to grow up to be masculine, dress him in shades of red or pink; if you hoped for your little girl to grow up feminine, dress her in blue

There were also many other claims about blue is suitable for blond babies and pink is better for brunettes, or blue is for blue-eyed babies and pink is for brown-eyed babies etc.

At that time, there was no one unified rule for which color signifies which gender yet.

So when did pink for girls and blue for boys took over?

During the 1940s, US manufacturers and retailers seem to settle on one "rule" and promoted the idea of blue for boys and pink for girls.

This kind of stereotype was once challenged during the late 60s and 70s due to women's liberation movement, the fad came right back in the mid 80s with the development of prenatal testing.

By promoting color-gender stereotype, manufacturers and retailers could encourage parents, who might have already have enough baby products due to their previous child, to buy a whole new set of products just to fit the baby's gender.

Even though unisex is the big trend now, the mind of associating pink with girls and blue with boys seem to deep-rooted in many people's minds.

According to the “red dress effect” people wearing red are more attractive to the opposite sex.

Wear red on your first date!

If you're wondering what color to buy a new outfit in, red could just make a great choice.

Why? According to the theory of the "red dress effect", people wearing red are perceived to be more sexually appealing than those wearing other colors.

While there is not enough scientific research to prove this theory, experiments have shown that men are more attracted to women wearing a red dress than any other color, even if it's the same woman in the dress. It doesn't even have to be a garment that is "sexy" or revealing – a red t-shirt should do the trick.

One theory for this phenomenon is the behavior of animals. The face, chest, and genitalia of female primates turn red to sexually attract males, and being close relatives to primates, humans may also instinctively associate red with being sexually available, too.

Research also shows that females may be more attracted to men wearing red, as it indicates the dominant power and high status of an alpha male.

Surgeons can become desensitized when staring at blood for a very long time, while green and blue can refresh their eyesight.

Why do surgeons wear green scrub instead of white?

Medics wear white coat for most of the time.

Medics wear blue or green scrub during surgery.

You might already know that doctors and nurses wear white, for recognition, status and cleanliness. But do you know why surgeon medics wear blue and green?

It all comes down to helping enhance the surgeon's sight.

During surgery, the surgeon will be staring at the flesh, blood and organs of a patient for an extended period of time. Our brain interprets these colors as relative to each other and in turn will weaken the signal for red. This can cause the surgeon to become desensitized, making it harder to see small details between the two colors.

Glancing up during surgery to see green or blue uniforms can help refresh signals in the brain and improve the doctor's performance.

Staring at red colors for long periods can lead to green illusions when shifting his or her sight to something white, which can be very distracting. When surgeons glance at the scrubs, the green illusion blends in and becomes less noticeable.

So while white is considered the color of cleanliness, green and blue are still the best uniform choice for surgeons.

Who decided wedding dresses should be white?

Queen Victoria's taste in wedding dresses kick-started the white gown trend.

In Western culture, a white wedding dress is seen as a traditional choice. But have you ever questioned when and how the "white wedding" became a common practice?

It was Queen Victoria in 1840 who kickstarted the trend by wearing a white dress to her wedding, claiming the color accentuated the lace detailing on the gown.

On her orders, ensuring that she was the focus on the day, no other guest could wear white to the wedding.

Her taste set the standard for wedding dresses, and from then onwards, the angelic shade has remained the primary color of choice for Western ceremonies.

What did brides wear at their weddings before 1840?

Before Queen Victoria's wedding, gold and silver were a common choice for royal brides.

As for ordinary people in Europe, brides would wear their best dress on their wedding day, no matter what color.

This was a very practical choice because it could be worn to other occasions, and it is far more cost effective than buying something new.

White, on the other hand, was a very uncommon choice, as only wealthy families could afford to keep the easily-stained dress clean.

Did you know?
In the United Kingdom, a bride has another set of traditions to follow – she must carry items for luck and protection. An old English nursery rhyme sums up the requirements: "something old, something new, something borrowed, something blue, and a silver sixpence in her shoe."

Why are suits and tuxedos always in black?

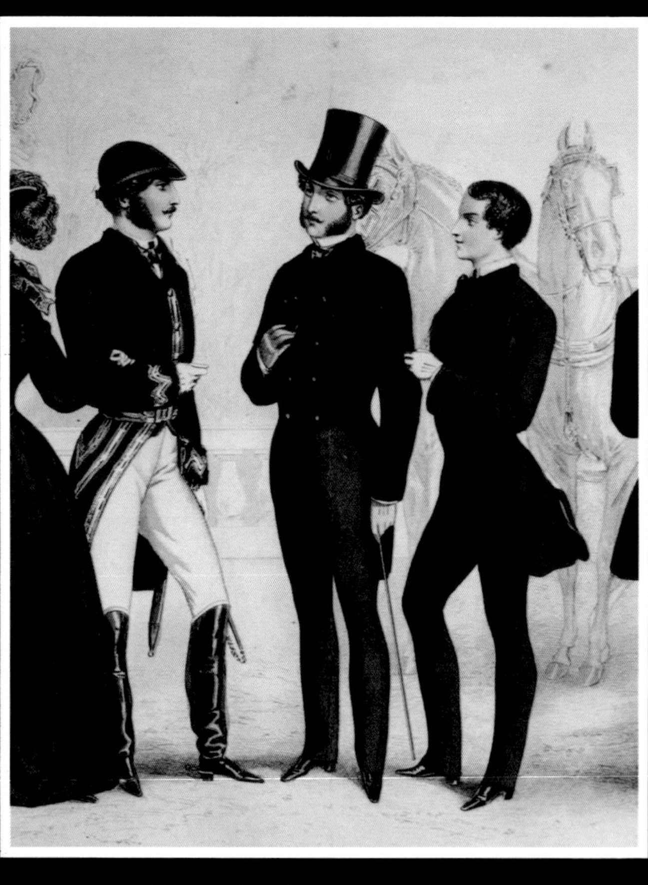

Suits and tuxedos are always in black.

Black is the most popular color choice for formalwear for both men and women. Why? Aside from personal preferences, there are a few different explanations, although no definite answers.

The likely conclusion is that multiple factors over history has lead to creating this trend. Let's look at three popular theories:

Black is an indicator of wealth

During medieval times, wearing black was a sign of wealth and social status as true black fabric was extremely expensive and difficult to produce.

By the end of the century, advancements in dye skills meant it was easier to manufacture true black and the trend for wearing the color spread from Italy to other parts of the world. The shade became popular with foreign kings, princes, nobles, and royals for many centuries onwards.

A country mourned with the Queen

After the death of Prince Albert, Queen Victoria decreed that everyone in the household had to appear in full mourning while on duty for two years.

The whole country, even those in the poorest rural cottages, wore black to mourn his passing. Even the Queen herself wore black for the rest of her life.

Out of respect, or perhaps to be politically correct, other nobles and people of middle class followed her example.

Black is practical

During the industrial revolution, burning coal made the air thick with soot and smoke. As any other color would blacken easily when exposed to the dirty air, men chose to wear the dark shade to work everyday for practicality.

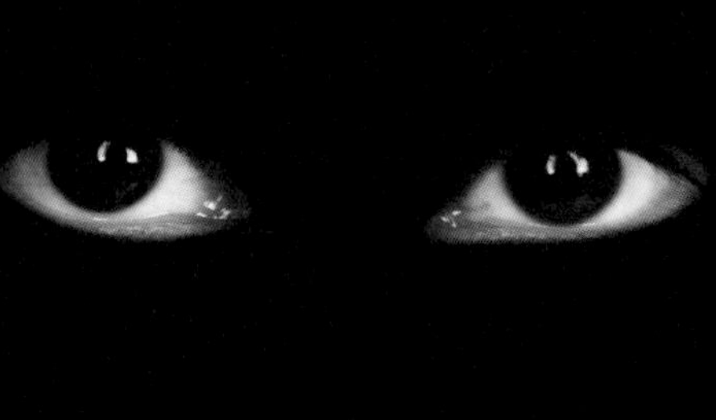

Real ninjas don't wear black

The word "ninja" will conjure a very vivid picture for most people: a shadowed figure in a black suit with a face covered by a mask. This is an image formed from years of film and media portrayals, but in fact, this depiction might not be accurate.

To understand a ninja you must know his purpose: He was a spy for the king, an assassin, collecting intelligence and acting as a shadow and a secret agent.

Why would a ninja wear something so conspicuous when he's trying to blend into the crowd to get close to his target? Surely wearing an all-black uniform with a mask would draw attention during the day?

Even at night, black isn't the most intelligent choice. If a ninja is on an outdoor mission, black can be seen as a shadow.

Navy and dark purple are, in fact, a closer color to the night sky, while dark brown is the closest color to the ground. It's unlikely you'll see a ninja in real life, so you might just have to believe us on this one.

Did you know?
A ninja's clothing is double-sided, with each side being a different color. Why? If they are exposed and chased, they can switch clothing inside out to mislead and escape the enemy.

All kinds of collars, all kinds of work

You've probably used the terms "white collar" and "blue collar" to describe different classes of workers, but did you know there are four more collar-related terms that are much less frequently used?

Let's look at all of them:

White collar
Represents the workers who often wear white shirts to work, such as office workers, administrators, management teams, and those who do paperwork.

Blue collar
Represents the color of blue jeans or chambray worn by the "working class", such as factory workers, miners and structural workers.

Pink collar
First coined in the 1970s to describe those who did secretarial work (predominantly a role filled by women). Later it began being used to describe care-oriented careers, such as nurses, teachers and childminders.

Gray collar
Represents professionally trained workers with higher qualifications than blue collar workers, such as an engineer and high-technology technicians.

Gold collar
Represents highly-trained and skilled workers valued for their innovation, independence, and intelligence, such as doctors, lawyers, scientists.

Green collar
Represents environmental sector workers and jobs related to sustainability, such as organic farmers and eco-friendly engineers.

Yet these classifications may overlap each other, as some terms were newly developed to further describe their characteristics.

Colors killing you slowly

Emerald green and Perkin's purple were deadly colors in the 1860s

In nature, bright colors are a sign of poison - a protective mechanism for small animals and plants, warning predators to stay away. When it comes to fashion, it turns out bright colors can be just as deadly, too.

Emerald Green

In 1814, Wilhelm Dye and White Lead Company in Germany developed a new green dye, the dazzling jewel shade was named "Emerald green" and was much admired by the public.

Its desirability meant it was quickly used across many products, including clothing. But as people were exposed to the dye for extended periods of time, they started to fall ill in dramatic ways - vomiting blood, shedding hair, showing up with skin sores and even experiencing liver and kidney failure. The culprit? Arsenic poisoning.

In the late 1860s the poisonous Emerald green finally went out of fashion. You would think that would be the end of poison in dyes but unfortunately, another deadly jewel tone from England had already come into vogue during the 1860s.

Mauveine

This time it was a red-purple shade called Mauveine, or Perkin's purple, created from an aniline compound.

Once again this widely used color was found to be poisonous, with people exposed to the dye suffering severe repercussions caused by aniline, including respiratory diseases, measles and amputation due to blood poisoning and cancer.

By the end of the 19th century, people started to believe it was the color dye making them sick, this time people learned the lesson and avoided bright colors. Even today, some companies advertise their clothing as using natural dye, which is completely safe for humans to wear.

FACTS ABOUT OUTER

The first cardigan was a knitted waistcoat worn by the Earl of Cardigan during war.

Cardigans used to be military wear

Who knew cardigan are often portrayed in society as something ordinary and boring, worn by librarians, grandmas and "nerds", would have been "born" on the battlefield?

Turns out the knitwear was named after the 7th Earl of Cardigan, who had lead the Light Brigade into the battle of Balaclava wearing a knitted waistcoat because that day was unusually cold.

In celebration of his safe return, his countrymen celebrated both his achievements and his fashion choice. His knitted waistcoat became commercially produced and named the "cardigan" after the Earl. Later, the term was used to describe knitted garments with front openings.

So how did the waistcoat-like cardigan come to resemble what we know today?

The credit goes to Coco Chanel! She was frustrated that her hair would be messed up every time she removed men's sweaters with tight necklines. So she cut a normal men's sweater down the front and, voila! The modern cardigan was born.

Henry Hood, Coxswain of the Seaton Carew Lifeboat, wears an RNLI cork life jacket, c. 1800s.

The life jacket that looks like a bomb vest

With synthetic material not invented until the 1930s, have you ever wondered what the first life jacket in 1765 was made of?

The answer may surprise you – it's cork!

Far from the light life jackets we know today, cork is solid and cumbersome. Despite its appearance – which can look a little terrifying, like explosives strapped to one's body – the buoyancy of the wood made for a great primitive life jacket.

The need for cork life jackets didn't, in fact, arrive until iron ships came into production.

Prior to that, the ships were made of wood and should an accident happen, the wooden debris would provide ample opportunities for passengers to find something to cling onto until help arrived.

It was the tragedy of the Titanic that finally put in place the first official regulations for life jackets; the first International Convention for the Safety of Life at Sea was held in 1913, ensuring that future ships would carry life jackets for safety.

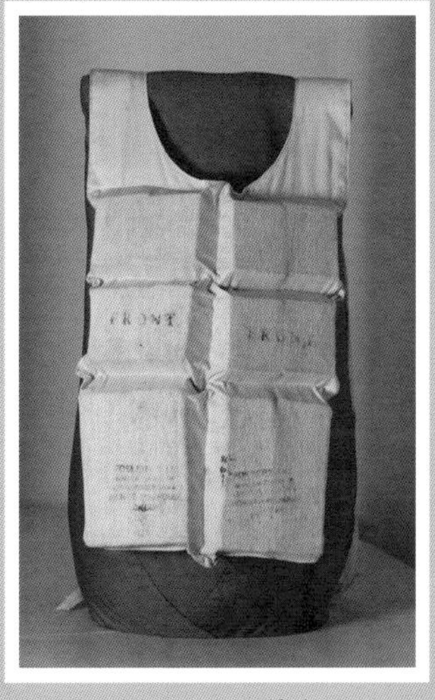

Titanic's survivor life jacket

Why you might not want to rely on that bulletproof vest

A bulletproof vest designed by Jan Szczepanik was tested with a 7 mm revolver, fired at a person wearing the vest in 1901.

Hopefully you will never be in need of a bulletproof vest. But if you are, it may not be the answer to all your problems.

Other than the obvious issue that it only covers vital organs in the chest and abdomen, the vest itself doesn't always stop a flying bullet.

General bulletproof vests are made from a material called Kevlar. Acting like a net stopping a football, the layers of Kevlar slows down the bullet, but if the layers are already damaged, or the bullet flies too fast, a bullet could still penetrate Kevlar.

<u>No match for a rifle</u>
In general, rifle bullets fly much faster than pistol bullets. The vest might block a .44 magnum handgun but the power of a rifle will rip through it.

<u>It only protects from one bullet</u>
Once a bullet has hit a vest, the fibers at that spot are already damaged and provides no protection. You must replace the ballistic material before wearing it again.

<u>It can't get wet</u>
Water could be a good lubricant reducing friction between the bullet and the vest, letting the bullet pass through the fiber easily. Look for specific waterproof models if needed.

<u>It has an expiry date</u>
The ballistic material will weaken and degrade over time, rendering the vest useless if left for a long period.

<u>It's still going to hurt</u>
The impact of a bullet, even if it doesn't penetrate the vest, can cause a serious amount of pain and bruising.

<u>No match for a knife</u>
You might be safe from a bullet but the stabbing motion from a knife will penetrate the vest.

Simply speaking, there is no actual bullet "proof" vest – it's actually a bullet-resistant vest at most. If you're going to be needing one, you should do more research and understand exactly what your bulletproof vest can and cannot do.

Inuit's natural Gore-Tex coat

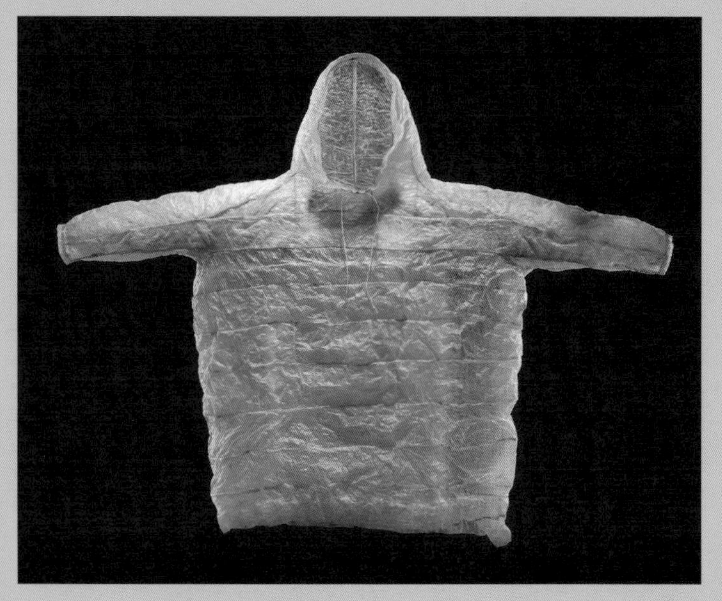

An Inuit gut parka made of a whale's gut.

Long before the invention of the innovative waterproof fabric Gore-Tex in 1969, a natural solution already existed.

Lightweight, thin, waterproof and breathable: it was a primitive alternative to modern Gore-Tex technology. Who would have known it was made of animal guts!

The harsh conditions and extreme weather of the Arctic region meant the Inuit people – an indigenous group inhabiting the region – needed to develop smart outerwear solutions to survive.

Rather than waste any resources, the Inuits would use animals gastrointestinal tracts and bones to create gut parkas as raincoats. The structure of the organ met many essential needs: it was breathable, durable, and wouldn't freeze or crack easily in extreme environments, which the Inuits would wear them when kayaking or fishing in shallow tidal waters.

How would the raincoat be made?

Once an animal was hunted, often a whale or a seal, it would be gutted, the intestines removed, cleaned and left outside. The cold transformed the intestines into an opaque material that could be used as a fabric and cut and sewn into the shape of a parka.

To make sure the parka was fully waterproof, the bones of the animals were rendered down into a glue, helping seal the seams. Once the process was complete, the parka would be filled up with water to test its effectiveness.

Why is a waterproof and breathable jacket so important in the Arctic?

In sub-zero conditions, staying dry is as important as keeping warm, as water turns to ice in such cold temperatures.

Being waterproof protects from the elements externally, while having a jacket that is breathable allows sweat to escape from the inside. If it doesn't, sweat would start to condense inside your clothes and cool down your body temperature rapidly and you could be in danger of freezing to death.

Smoking jacket was made to protect your pretty clothes from smoke smell.

One jacket to keep smoke out of your pretty clothes

Cigarette smoke – and in particular the stale cigarette smoke that's found in bars and restaurants without proper ventilation – can linger on clothing, making it difficult to remove.

This problem isn't a new one — it was first brought to everyone's attention in England in the 1850s, when the Turkish tobacco industry was booming and smoking became popular. The British gentlemen of the time found a practical fashion solution for the pesky problem: the "smoking jacket".

Designed with thick velvet, it looked like luxurious leisurewear but the plush fabric served the added purpose of preventing smoke clinging to clothing.

Since then, the smoking jacket has gone through several design changes, the most notable being the introduction of a more formal version of the jacket.

Made from heavier material and featuring one button, it's become a fashionable choice for "black-tie optional" events and parties, such as the Academy Awards, holiday parties, the ballet, or simply for going out on the town.

Peter Cook in a leather biker jacket.

Why is the zipper on a biker jacket always diagonal?

Have you ever noticed that classic leather biker jackets always feature an asymmetrical front closure? You might just think it's a decision based on style but, in fact, it's all about function.

The first ever leather jacket was actually a flight jacket fastened with buttons. Then, in 1928, the now iconic American motorcycle manufacturer Harley Davidson released the very first biker jacket which featured zippers.

The reason for the switch of fastening type was to help the wearer to take off and put on the outerwear with increased speed and ease. The diagonal zipper position was chosen to give a better fit.

Why? Zips that are vertically placed can bunch up on the body if the wearer leans forward but a slightly diagonal zipper won't.

The result was a simple yet ingenious design detail that has since stood the test of time.

4 Things you don't know about MA-1

If you walk down the street in any big city today, you'll surely spot someone wearing a MA-1 bomber jacket. Functional and stylish, the garment has become a popular piece of streetwear. But are you aware of its origin?

The MA-1 was inspired by military wear — flight jackets, to be exact. During the 1940s and 1950s, the US Air Force created the jacket with plenty of functional style details to help them in flight.

What features make the classic MA-1 jacket?

Color with purpose
The sage green exterior was selected as a camouflage color. The orange lining inside the jacket serves as a rescue signal. In case of an emergency, the pilot can reverse the jacket to expose the orange side in the hopes of being spotted.

Handy utility pockets
The tiny cockpits of the plane doesn't allow much room to move and store things, so the jacket was designed with a pocket on the left-hand side called cigarette or utility pocket, that could also be used to hold pens.

Intelligent fabric choices
Airplane cabins during WW2 were not pressurized, meaning it was terribly cold at high altitudes. This is why the body of the jacket is made from nylon fabric which is both light and warm. The cuffs and collar were knitted to contain body warmth and keep out the freezing cold air.

Functional straps
A traditional bomber jacket had front tapes near chest were to secure a pilot's air mask, tubes and wires in place, yet it is no longer needed as modern plane cabins are pressurized.

Today, flight suits and jackets are made from lightweight and fire-resistant material, MA-1 jackets are no longer worn by pilots, but adopted by civilians as a fashion item.

Why were soldiers allowed to paint sexy women on their uniform?

A collection of jackets featuring sexy pin-up girls worn by WWII pilots.

During WW2, it was common to see air force soldiers wearing bomber jackets covered in prints and patches including provocative pin-up girls, cartoon characters and charms.

With the army being known for its strict uniform regulations, this period was the only one in history when this was surprisingly relaxed.

This type of art is called "nose art". The style was first painted on planes as an outlet for pilots to express themselves, identify friendly units and provide psychological support against the stress of war.

According to historian John Conway, air force pilots were often at the young age of 18 or 19, and most of them were far away from home for the first time. The images of cartoon characters and pin-up girls which they grew up with could evoke good memories from home and peaceful times.

Soon, pilots applied nose art to their bomber jackets, which wasn't reprimanded by the army.

Why?

It was like offering "The Last Supper" to the pilots, as these young men were serving their country in one of the most dangerous professions and periods in history.

At the worst of times, pilots were expected a 1 in 15 chance of being shot down. The army – knowing that they were at high risk of losing their lives – would rather let them enjoy small pleasures, such as a joyful jacket when they could, and only focus on enforcing regulations and rules that actually mattered.

Sukajan jacket: From a soldier's souvenir to street fashion

An early 1950s-style sukajan jacket with a dragon head and gold eagle embroidery on the outside and inside.

The silk bomber jackets today typically feature beautiful embroidered illustrations of motifs. While they may just seem like a fashionable piece of clothing, there's a history behind their creation.

The jackets, a blend of East and West, are often called souvenir jackets or "sukajans". They were created for soldiers in the United States Force Japan as souvenirs, in order to honor their time in the country after the end of WW2.

A US sailor wearing a "Tiger" sukajan jacket in a Japan tailor store, hunting for another souvenirs in the mid-1950s.

Embroidery craftsmen (also known as "nuiko"), are still using vintage embroidery machines to keep their rich tradition alive.

While soldiers were hunting for traditional Japanese items, such as Kimono, as tokens of their travels, local tailors from Kosho & Co. came up with the idea of creating a bomber jacket made with silk featuring traditional Japanese embroidery.

The jacket was embroidered inside and out with colorful and meaningful motifs, such as maps, eagles, geishas or dragons symbolizing the incorporation of US and Japan.

As demand took off to replicate the soldiers' jackets, local tailors would use old silk parachutes to create Sukajan jackets.

A Coat with 11 Functions

A trench coat is a classic wardrobe staple that many of us already own, with a design that has changed remarkably little over the past 100 years.

Trench coat was originally designed as a military coat, only worn by British officers in WW1. On returning home to their civilian lives, veterans continued to wear it proudly as a reminder of the heroic battles fought.

What were the features on a trench coat, and why were they originally designed?

1. Napoleonic collar
It can be popped up and turned over to protect the wearer from rain and wind.

2. Hook and eye
Quick fastening for closing the collar.

3. Throat latch
Used to reinforce the standing collar.

4. Epaulettes
Used to hook on accessories that needed to be easily accessible, such as binoculars, gloves, whistles and gas masks.

5. D-ring belt
Used to fasten important items to the waist, such as firearms, swords, grenades and maps.

6. Gun flap
Used to stop rain entering the jacket when firing a rifle.

7. Storm pocket
A pocket that can be reached from both inside and outside of the coat, which can be buttoned to keep out the rain.

8. Cuff straps
Used to strap items, such as maps, to the wrist. They also keep rain out when tightened.

9. Removable lining
Insulated, detachable lining which can be used as a blanket.

10. Back flap yoke
Adding breathability at the rear of the coat.

11. Wedge back vent
Providing extra mobility.

So next time you put on your favorite trench coat, you might find yourself appreciating the garment's detailing for more than just its looks!

Suit jacket
Blazer

Blazer vs. suit jacket: What are the differences?

How to tell the difference between a suit jacket and a blazer?

Most people wouldn't be able to distinguish the difference between a suit jacket and a blazer but there are some key contrasts.

What is a suit jacket?

A suit jacket is a formalwear jacket with matching pants. It is often produced in finer materials such as cotton, linen or worsted wool. The suit jacket has a closer fit than a blazer and is designed to be worn with only a dress shirt underneath.

What is a blazer?

More casual than a suit jacket, a traditional blazer is commonly made of wool and often features contrast color piping and brass buttons.

Modern blazers, on the other hand, look exactly like suit jackets but usually have a generous fit to allow them to be worn over bulkier garments like sweaters, and they do not come with matching pants.

Can a suit jacket be worn as a blazer?

It can, as long as you wear it with non-matching pants.
Just keep in mind that because the suit jacket is part of a set, if you wash and wear only the jacket regularly you'll fade the fabric and no longer have a matching pair of pants.

The suit buttoning etiquette exists because King Edward VII had a large belly

If you are a man with a formal occasion to go to, it's not quite enough to just throw on any suit and head out the door.

Pay attention and you will notice some gentlemen will undo their suit jacket when sitting, while some will not, it is a part of menswear etiquette, and the rules vary due to the types of jacket and the wearer's actions.

We have King Edward VII to thank for these quirky dressing rules. During the early 1900s, the King had trouble buttoning the last button on his waistcoat due to his rather round belly.

To keep from offending the royal leader, his followers also left the last button undone. As the influence of Britain globally at the time was so strong, the trend spread to other parts of the world, too.

Meanwhile, lounge suits in the early 20th century were relatively casual and gentlemen started to replace tradition riding coats with lounge suits.

When riding on horseback, people found that unfastening the last button can control the jacket drape properly without puckering. Therefore unfastening jacket buttons while sitting is also a practical etiquette.

So, what are the different button styles of jackets?

1-button suit
Keep buttoned up when standing, and unfastened when sitting.

2-button suit
Top button remains buttoned when standing, unfastened when sitting, and always keep the last button undone.

3-button suit
When standing, it is optional to fasten the top button, always fasten the second button, and leave the last one undone. Unbutton every button when sitting.

Double-breasted suit
Fasten every button except the last button next to the opening of the jacket.

Regardless of whether you're sitting or standing, keep the suit buttoned until you take the jacket off.

Waistcoat
Always unbutton the last button.

Why are there white stitches on my suit?

Marks you would want to remove from your suit.

Isn't it the epitome of luxury to have a bespoke suit created and custom fit for your every need? So why do some suits have white stitches left on the garment? After all that expense, did the tailor forget to finish the job properly? The reason is, in fact, the opposite.

The white stitches are called baste stitches.

During fitting and construction, these baste stitches are used to temporarily secure sections of the suit and ensure any loose parts, such as lapel and vents, won't get caught on something during packaging or transportation.

They are also sometimes used as a sign of a suit having been handmade using fine craftsmanship, showing off the fact that the suit is not a mass production product.

Still, that does not mean you should walk around with those stitches and marks on display. Remove them or you might risk looking like a menswear amateur!

What are the common removable tailoring elements?

<u>The pick stitching on the vent and lapel notch</u>
The pick stitching, usually a white cross stitch, on the lapel and vent keeps the garment neat and wrinkle-free.

<u>The brand tag on the sleeve</u>
Used by the production factory or shop owners to identify a suit, the tag is stitched into the suit cuff and can be removed before wear.

<u>The sewn-up pockets</u>
These are used to ensure the pocket sits neatly and stays clean. If there is a flap to cover it up and you want to keep things perfectly neat, it is okay to leave it there.

Why does a lapel have a buttonhole, when there is no matching button?

For every buttonhole, there's a matching button. That's the obvious conclusion, but is it true?

The answer is surprisingly no. Some suits feature buttonholes on the left lapel with no corresponding button on the right lapel.

A functional garment detail, originating from coats and jackets, traditionally had a button underneath the lapel. This allowed the wearer to turn up the collar and fasten it around the neck, keeping out the cold.

Slowly, suit jacket lapels have become more about fashion than function, with buttons removed and only some suits keeping the buttonhole.

This doesn't mean every extra buttonhole is completely useless - they do get a spin at red carpet events when a boutonniere, or small bouquet of flowers, is held in place through the hole.

Did you know?
In the 1940s, the buttonhole may have been used to attach a hat. By holding the hat in place with a piece of cord and a button, it was a guarantee the hat wouldn't be blown around in the wind.

Suit cuff buttons and opening were first made for surgeon doctors.

A suit jacket's cuff opening was made for doctors

If you examine a suit jacket you'll see there's an opening on the cuffs. It might seem like a fashion detail, but in truth, they were first created to serve a functional purpose.

Military field doctors in the early 19th century were always required to be dressed in suits, even on duty in the middle of battle.

Clearly not a job for a jacket of any old kind, Savile Row tailors in London created an opening on the cuff, helping doctors roll up their sleeves more easily without taking off their jackets.

The design was called "surgeon cuffs" and they still exist to this day — although thankfully they are no longer intended for use on the battlefield.

KISSING STACKED

KISSING NON-STACKED

Did you know?
There is an imperfect cuff button style called "kissing buttons". Often featured in Italian-style suits, the buttons touch and slightly overlap each other.

As the buttons are not perfectly aligned, this implies the suit is handmade by tailors instead of mass-produced.

The extra pocket keeps men from being hassled

How many pockets could we possibly need in a jacket? Instead of the standard two pockets, some suit jackets have three, with an extra one placed on the right-hand side.

It's a functional detail that started before the industrial revolution. Called the "ticket pocket" or "change pocket", it gave men who rode on horseback easy access to coins at toll booths without the hassle of reaching into their jacket.

After the industrial revolution, the trend remained. However, instead of men on horseback, it was men who needed quick access to their train tickets during the rush of the daily commute.

Did you know?
It may have originated as a British invention, but the style detail is also found on Italian and American suits, too.

Former First Lady Jackie O, who was wearing a strawberry pink Chanel suit on the day her husband was assassinated in November 22, 1963.

The pink suit that shocked America

Jacqueline Onassis Kennedy (Jackie) was one of the most influential fashion icons of her time. From the pillbox hat to oversized sunglasses, elbow-length white gloves and stylish head scarves...her wardrobe and chic style have inspired millions. Yet her most famous look, a strawberry pink Chanel suit and matching pillbox hat, comes with a deadly tale.

In 1963, one of the most infamous and brutal assassinations in American history, the death of John F. Kennedy (JFK) happened during a visit to Dallas, Texas. Jackie, who wore the pink suit on that day, was sitting right next to her husband when he was shot and killed, and JFK's blood was splattered all over her.

The scene was shocking, but she refused to change or clean the blood on her suit. She kept wearing the suit, a particular favorite of her husband, in public that day — even while Vice President Johnson took the Oath of Office as president. She created a startling scene saying "I want them to see what they have done to Jack (JFK)."

The blood-stained suit was then cited as "the most legendary garment in American history", as it represents an assassination and a national nightmare.

The suit was never cleaned and stored with a note of JFK's death "November, 22nd,1963".

While the matching pink pillbox hat was lost right after the assassination, the suit is now preserved out of the public's view in the National Archive and Records Administration (NARA) Building in Maryland, the United States.

FACTS ABOUT TOP

A bear in a wife beater.

A garment of violence: WIFE BEATER!

How did the ubiquitous white tank top get saddled with such a violent nickname "wife beater"?

The term "wife beater" was popularized after a man violently beat his wife to death in Detroit in 1947. A photo of the murderer wearing a white stained tank top captioned "The Wife-Beater" started to circulate.

Since then the image of the dirty white tank or undershirt is something you may be familiar with from TV and movies – the piece of clothing is often seen on characters portraying abusive violent husbands, reminiscent of the famous photograph.

One of the iconic images was Marlon Brando's portrayal of Stanley Kowalski in the movie A Streetcar Named Desire, who wore a dirty white tank top and had a violent and irritated personality.

Did you know?
There is a "wife beater" beer!

Stella Artois, a Belgium beer company producing a beer with a higher alcohol content than competitors, was given the nickname "wife beater". The higher alcohol content in the beer resulted in people getting drunk quickly, sometimes leading to aggressive behavior and domestic violence.

Mermaid Club, Philadelphia" members in tank suits, c. 1915-1920.

What does the “tank” have to do with a tank top?

Did you know the sleeveless tank top was once seen as immodest, and that it was actually once swimwear?

Much like the swimsuit was named after the swimming pool, the tank was named after the swimming tank – which was the name for swimming pools in the 1920s. (This is also how the term “tank suit” was popularized.)

At first, the garment was only worn as an undershirt. It was Hollywood movies, most famously A Streetcar Named Desire, that started changing people’s perception of wearing the garment in public during the 1950s.

Prior to then, it was not common for a woman to show her bare arms in public, so when women started to participate in the Olympic Games in Stockholm, Sweden, in 1912, the “tank suits” they were wearing were viewed by the media and public as immodest.

During the 1970s, the perspective of the tank top started to change. It became more acceptable for both men and women to wear the garment in public within the Western world.

As fitness and health started to trend, people began wearing a tank top, sometimes with a jacket over the top, to go outside and exercise. Slowly it became a fashionable item, and today it is one of the most common garments in our wardrobe.

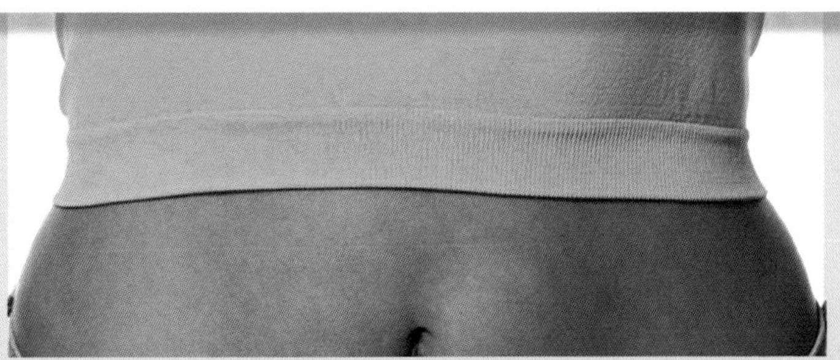

Turns out, the tube top is a million dollar business!

Fashion's million dollar fabric scraps

The tube top – not a particularly functional piece of clothing but popular as a way to show off a toned midsection – was actually worn centuries ago for practical purposes in Ancient Greece.

It was a fabric wrapped around women's chests in offer of support and modesty. Later it changed from a practical piece of fabric into an iconic clothing item – a great example of how a good eye can usher in a new era of fashion.

This man with a good eye and good business sense was Iranian Israeli fashion designer Elie Tahari. He discovered tubes of fabric in a store in New York which were the result of a manufacturing error, and had a hunch that the faulty material would prove popular.

He bought the simple tubes of fabric at the price of $2, held in place with elastic, and resold them for $3 - $4.

After smuggling them into a trade show his success grew, resulting in thousands of orders in one day, and a reason to start his own label.

Tahari expanded his business and, as well as manufacturing tube tops in 1973, moved into designing dresses and halter tops, both key pieces of 1970s disco fashion.

T-shirt =
Tea shirt?

Available in a range of price-points and fabrics, the classic t-shirt is the one piece of clothing nearly every man or woman owns. But, have you ever stopped to think about the origins of this humble wardrobe staple?

The t-shirt was, in fact, initially a piece of underwear worn by sailors and marines.

One theory of how it got its name is that during the 1600s workers were unloading tea on the docks of Maryland in America while wearing a simple slip-on crew necked shirt, which was later named "tea shirt".

Another theory is the name was inspired, quite simply, by the piece of clothing's T-shaped silhouette.

Regardless of which theory is true, we do know the t-shirt has become an incredibly popular wardrobe mainstay today.

Did you know?

The earliest known recorded use of the word "t-shirt" is from popular author F. Scott Fitzgerald's novel The Side of Paradise, published in 1920.

Why do Breton shirts have 21 stripes?

Did you know that the classic blue and white striped shirt, an item of clothing popular with hipsters, geeks and fashionistas, actually has a formal and strictly regimented origin?

The piece of clothing was originally a uniform worn by French Seamen in 1858 called the Breton. To qualify as a Breton top, the bands of color on the shirt needed to be 2cm white and 1cm blue with exactly 21 stripes of each color, representing the 21 naval victories of military leader Napoleon.

How has this sailors uniform become synonymous with chic French style today?

We can thank fashion designer Coco Chanel for that. She saw the sailors in their striped tops while on the Northern seasides of France and became inspired by the design.

Anything Coco Chanel wore made headlines and quickly the Breton striped tee became the symbol of French fashion – a style that is still unwaveringly popular today.

RIGHT: A traditional breton shirt has 21 stripes.

1
2
3
4
5
6
7
8
9
10
11
12
13
14
15
16
17
18
19
20
21

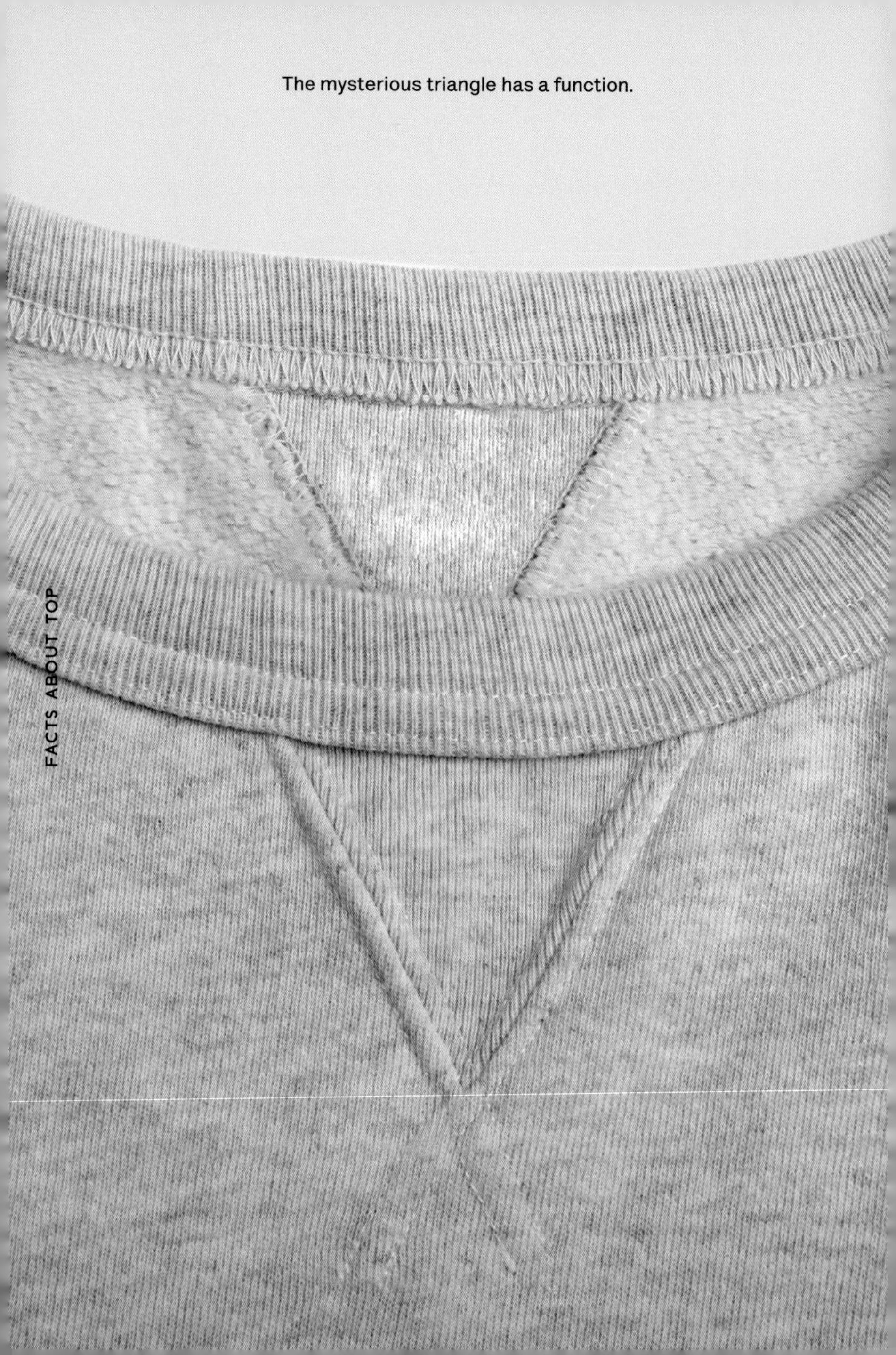

The mysterious triangle has a function.

The hidden sponge in your sweatshirt!

Most people have a sweatshirt, but how many of us have noticed the small triangular detail around the neck and knows what is it for?

The "triangular" part is actually a functional addition rather than just style. It is called a V-insert or V-stitch, made of thick, ribbed cotton jersey or elastic material piece of fabric.

It is used to absorb sweat like a sponge from the wearer's vigorous exercise, and prevent the neckline from tearing when it is being pulled over the head constantly due to its elastic property.

So next time you pull on a sweatshirt, maybe the sight of that V-insert could give you a little jolt of motivation to do some exercise!

Aloha! This casual shirt is courtroom-approved

Attorneys can wear aloha shirt in some of the courts in Hawaii.

You've probably assumed that the laid-back lifestyle and beautiful weather of Hawaii allows for a relaxed way of dressing. But have you ever heard of the phrase "Aloha Attire"?
It's the way to describe the dress code and Aloha shirts (aka Hawaiian shirts) unique to Hawaii – often worn as formalwear by government office workers, sometimes even attorneys in court.

These shirts are typically more understated than the loud Hawaiian print shirts favored by tourists and feature a reversed print.

The shirt is constructed with the printed side of the fabric facing inwards, making the colors more subtle and, in turn, the shirt more suitable for formal occasions.

The reverse print aloha shirt was promoted in 1962 by the Hawaiian Fashion Guild as a way to support the local garment industry, as well as show pride in the spirit of Hawaii and its unique relaxed lifestyle.

The practice was supported by the Hawaii Senate, which passed a resolution to support and encourage employees to wear Aloha Attire.

The dress codes of "Aloha Attire":

Aloha casual
Aloha button down shirt or polo tee, dressy shorts and sandals.

Aloha formal
Button down shirt, long pants, such as khaki pants, leather flip-flop sandals or sneakers.

Aloha crisp
Tucked in button down reverse print aloha shirt, dress pants with belt, sports coat and closed shoes or boat shoes.

Did you know?

The aloha shirt was first trademarked by Chinese merchants in the 1930s. During the Great Depression, when businesses were struggling, Chinese merchant Ellery Chun took over his father's clothing business in Hawaii.

He started to make short sleeve shirts using leftover fabrics from Japanese Kimonos and Yukatas. Typically bright and printed, these became the aloha shirt.

Contrast in the streets of London England Britain UK.

How did a white shirt reflect a man's social status?

Could the color of your shirt be a telltale sign of your social class? Maybe not in modern times, but if you lived during the 19th and 20th centuries there is a good chance it would have.

As the 19th century ushered in the era of formalwear, the white shirt was the epitome of high-class fashion for men.

Why? Because if you could keep a white shirt clean of 19th century-grime, especially the collar and cuffs, then it showed you were wealthy enough to avoid doing manual labor.

The colored shirt was introduced in the 20th century and became a popular choice with the lower class for the opposite reason – it was practical and hid the stains of physical work.

Today, while there is no doubt that a quality white shirt is a classic wardrobe staple, it's no longer a symbol of social status.

Why do some shirts have buttonholes in different directions?

The attention to detail in the construction of your shirt might be more impressive than you imagined. For example, did you know most dress shirts have two different kinds of buttonholes?

The collar and the very last button on a shirt are horizontal holes because these two buttons are the ones that do all the work; they have the biggest job resisting the movement in the shirt and need to have a little more room to shift around.

The buttons in-between the collar and the bottom of the shirt sit vertically because, with less movement in the body, the shirt buttons can simply remain centered.

Take a look at your own dress shirt. Can you spot two different kinds of buttonholes?

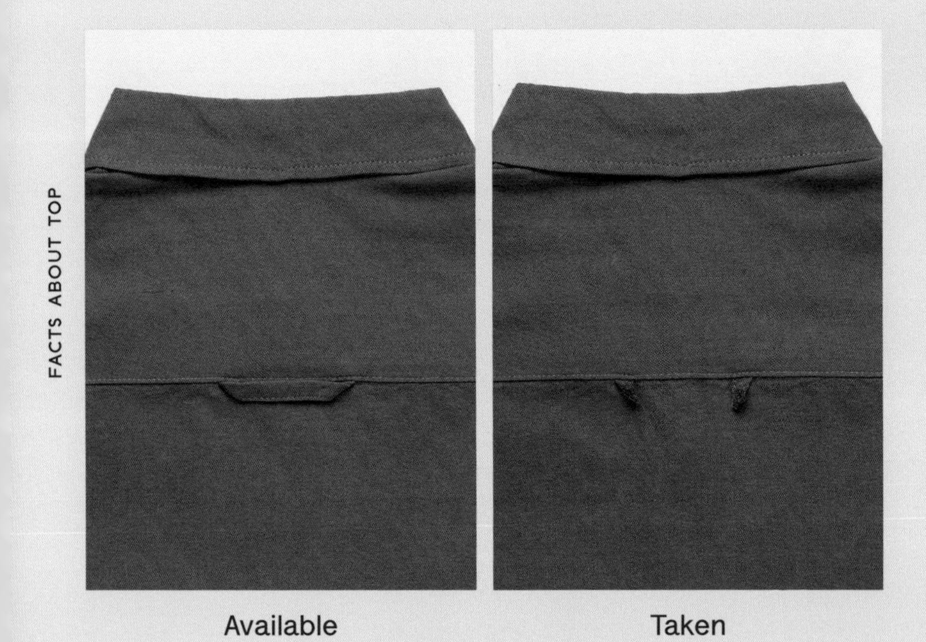

Available

Taken

Available or taken? Your shirt loop is a telltale sign

Need a signal to know if your crush considers you his girlfriend? Well, if your crush was an Ivy League student in the 1960s, you could always check the loop on the inside neck of his shirt to find out – a missing loop once meant the student in question was taken.

Of course, this gave girls a reason to cheekily remove the loop from the shirts of the boys they wanted to date.

This said, the primary reason for the shirt loop is, in fact, much more practical.

First conceived in the 1960s by menswear brand GANT, the shirt loop or "locker loop" was created to help Ivy League students hang their shirts in the locker room without getting them wrinkled, a trick inspired by a useful habit of sailors.

FACTS ABOUT BOTTOM

In North Korea, blue jeans equal to American imperialism.

No blue jeans in North Korea!

The humble blue jeans may be a classic working-class American icon, but according to the North Korea government, they are also an unacceptable piece of clothing.

The country considers the iconic garment a symbol of American imperialism, and has banned the item from being worn by citizens. In fact, North Koreans have been banned from wearing all Western garments.

The announcement was made in 2016 by North Korean news website Rimjin-gang. The areas most affected by these rules are the provinces bordering China, North Hamgyong and Yanggang, where the flow and access to information, trends and outside knowledge are harder to control.

The rule only applies to local citizens, meaning visitors to North Korea can wear their own Western clothes. However, if you're visiting memorials or official ceremonies it's best to skip the jeans and wear something else less controversial instead.

What is the tiny pouch inside your jeans' pocket for?

Did you know cowboys and miners inspired the functional details on your favorite pair of jeans? Let's take a look back at history to see how.

What is the smaller compartment on the inside of the front pocket?

Built into jeans on the unlikely request of cowboys, these miniature pockets were designed to hold pocket watches, as they were small and secure enough to protect the timepiece from getting broken.

What are the little copper studs for?

Jeans were originally designed for miners and laborers in the days of the American Gold Rush.

The tough work required a heavy duty fabric and construction to combat the stress of daily wear. Denim is a strong material but the stress points, such as pocket corners and the bottom of the button fly, needed reinforcements, so the copper rivets were then added for durability.

Bell bottom were first worn by sailors, not disco dancers!

When you think of bell bottom pants you may think of them on the dance floor but in fact, it was actually sailors who started the trend.

In the 17th century, sailors who were washing down the decks of ships were given bell bottoms to wear.

Why?

Because they could easily roll up the wide hem to keep the leg from getting wet.

How did the bell bottoms change from sailors uniform to a fashion sensation?

As the swinging 1960s ushered in the era of peace, love and second-hand clothing, the demand for surplus military clothing rose – and the second-hand navy bell bottoms become one of the most in-demand items.

In the 1970s, the release of the popular movie Saturday Night Fever (1977) made bell bottoms a true fashion sensation.

A group of women wearing pants doing Swedish gymnastics, c. 1900-1939.

The pants that promote women's rights

Before the 20th century, women wearing pants was considered both unfeminine and immodest due to the figure-hugging nature of the garment. Women were expected to wear large voluminous skirts that were impractical, heavy and cumbersome.

An early advocate of wearing trousers, Elizabeth Smith Miller, from America was the first reported women to wear Turkish pants to a women's rights convention held in New York. The ample fabric and roomy nature of the garment meant that there was less concern about immodesty.

Her neighbor, Amelia Bloomer, the women conspired to promote pants with a different angle. Rather than fight society's perception, why not change the focus to health?

The duo claimed the freedom of wearing pants allowed women to ride bikes, exercise and generally live a healthier lifestyle. The pants, called bloomers, had a modest amount of success but failed to change public perception at that time. It wasn't until WW2 that pants were truly acceptable or common for women to wear.

Cartoon of a woman wearing the bloomer costume.

WANTED
FOR WEARING PANTS

COCOCHANEL

IN BRETON SHIRTS & PANTS

Women wearing pants in Paris was technically illegal before 2013

Did you know, before 2013, if you were a woman wearing pants in Paris without permission from local police you were actually breaking the law?

Thankfully the 200-year-old decree, existing since the 1800s, has not been enforced for the last 50 years. The now-repealed ancient law stated that women in Paris must ask the permission of the local authorities to wear pants or risk imprisonment.

The law was put in place after the French Revolution, a period of social and political upheaval.

During that time, Parisian women fighting for equality made the controversial decision to wear pants. Napoleon, not happy with this symbol of equal opportunity, made a swift decree to ban all women in the fashion capital from continuing to do so.

The law was modified in the late 19th century for practical travel needs as pants could be worn when riding a bike or a horse on the streets of the city.

In 2013, the French government repealed the law and now women are "officially" allowed to wear pants in the French capital.

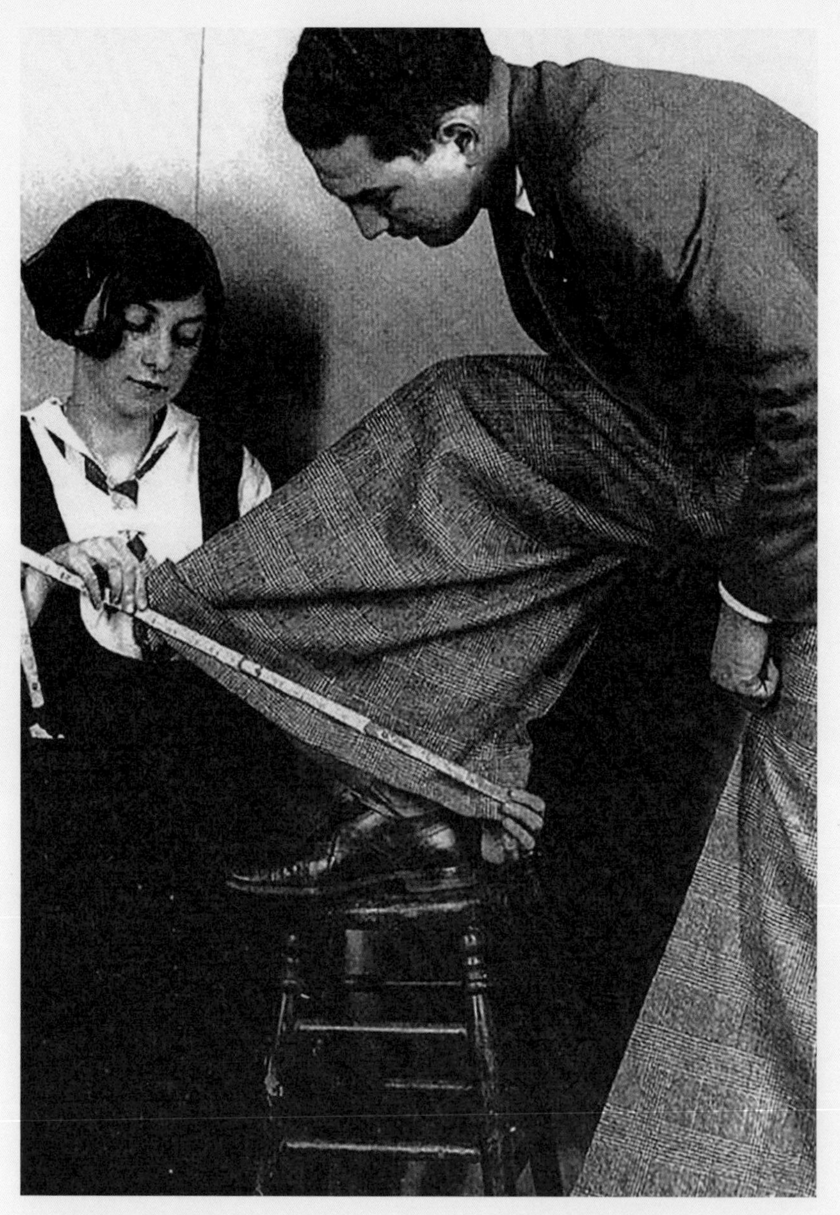

The hem circumference of Oxford bag could be as wide as 44cm, c. 1920.

Oxford bags are not bags

In history, there have been many questionable fashion choices, but "Oxford bags" – roomy, baggy men's slacks – might just be one of the more bizarre trends.

With a regular fit around the waist that expands down the leg to a very large cuff opening (measuring as wide as 44cm), the proportion made quite the statement.

Some believe the style was invented by students of the University of Oxford in the early 20th century to cover up "plus fours" – an equally unflattering pair of pants, similar to knickerbockers.

As you might imagine, wearing two pairs of baggy pants simultaneously was a rather unusual – and even more unflattering – choice.

Another, perhaps more probable, theory of the origin of the Oxford bags is that they were worn by the university's rowing club.

Rumored to originally be designed as warm-up pants, the extremely baggy leg and large opening cuff meant rowers could just slip the garment on and off without even removing their shoes.

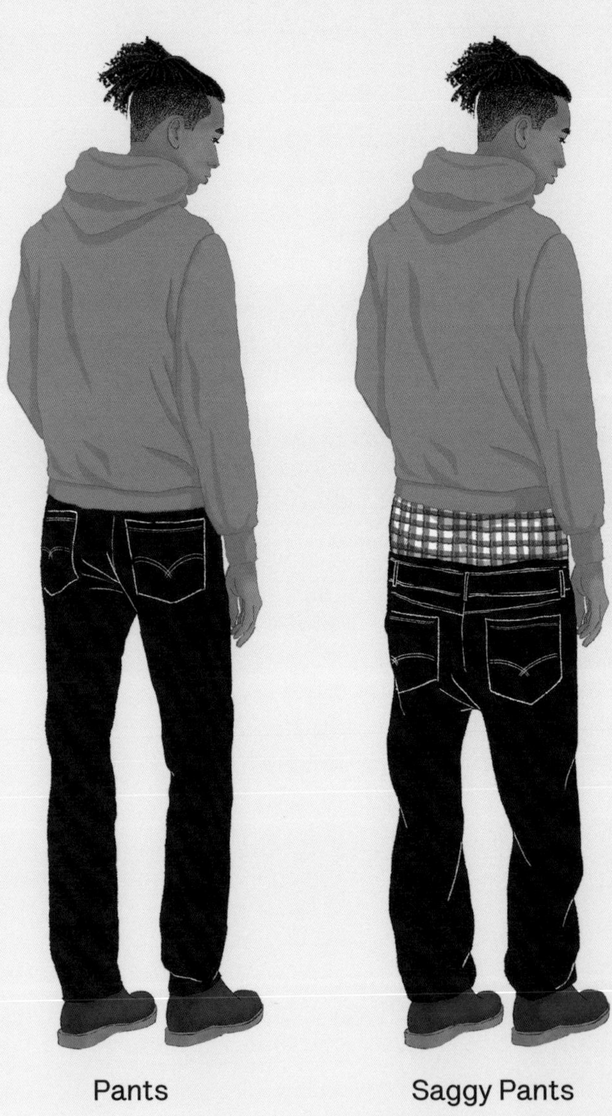

Pants

Saggy Pants

The "bad boy" way of wearing pants

You might have noticed that some men intentionally pull down their jeans to show off the elastic waistband of their underwear and consider it fashionable. This rebellious "bad boy" style of dressing, rather aptly, started in prison.

The uniform of inmates didn't always fit correctly and the lack of belts, which were not allowed because they could be used as a weapon, meant the uniform often hung down around the hips of inmates.

Once the inmates left prison, they took this fashion statement with them into the outside world.

In the 1990s the trend was catapulted into popular culture when a rapper wore low-slung jeans and exposed underwear in a music video, which caused many other rappers and teenagers to follow suit.

Did you know?

It has been rumored that if an inmate wears baggy pants, it is a sign he is either sexually available to other inmates, or that he was in a relationship with another inmate.

The crease on your suit pants was just an accident?!

Front crease usually appear on suit pants.

Have you ever noticed a crease down the front of some pants?

Called a "traveler's crease", it's usually found on semi-formal or formal pants. It exists for both fashion and function, adding sharpness to an ensemble, and making pants easy to fold and pack into garment bags or suitcases when traveling.

There are a couple of rumors about the origin of the pants crease, both which involve the British royal family.

One story tells the tale of King Edward VII taking shelter on a farm from the rain in a trip. To help dry his wet trousers the farmer and his wife pressed the King's pants, causing a defined crease on the front, and spurring a trend when the King was spotted shortly after in public.

The second story was that King Edward VII's rebellious son, King George V, challenged his father's normal style of wearing creases on the side of his pants, encouraging him to switch the crease to the front of his pants.

Yet none of these stories were documented clearly and are difficult to verify.

How to care for pants with a traveler's crease?

Wash pants as normal then iron, following the crease. If the pants don't have a permanent crease don't try to create one! It's specific to the design of the pants, and won't look quite the same on a different style of trousers.

Tight pants could be a man's worst nightmare!

While you might think labeling "tight pants on men" as a severe health hazard sounds silly, it is true! Here are three reasons wearing tight pants can be dangerous for men:

<u>Twisted testicles</u>
Overly tight or ill-fitting jeans that restrict the groin area can cause pain and twisted testicles. Worst case scenario? Testicles need to be removed!

<u>Infertility</u>
Sperm thrive in 2-4 degrees cooler than body temperature, but when wearing tight pants, testicles are pushed nearer to the body and being warmed up, causing sperm count to drop. If the situation continues, this can cause adverse long term effects sperm quality as well.

<u>Bladder weakness</u>
Wearing tight pants for a prolonged time can lead to an overactive bladder, meaning the muscles over-contract, constantly creating sudden urges to urinate, and can even cause urine leakage.

So next time you pull on your skintight jeans, you might want to think about replacing them up with some looser pants instead!

Did you know?

These three reasons are just a few examples of the severe health consequences of wearing overly tight pants. Other health issues such as bacterial and fungal infections are also very common among men and women wearing tight pants for a long time.

This dress could be the most dangerous fashion item ever!

A postcard shows a woman trying to climb over the fence with a hobble skirt.

Throughout history, women have suffered for fashion – cue beautiful but uncomfortable shoes, tight dresses, corsets, and heavy gowns. However, it was a particularly dangerous trend that began in the 1900s that has led to many serious injuries and death.

The garment was called the "hobble skirt" – named after the literal translation of how women were forced to walk awkwardly while wearing it.

The trend began innocently, based on the needs of the first female passenger to ever fly in a plane, Edith Hart O. Berg.

During a promotion exhibit held in France, Edith was getting into the open cabin of the aircraft when she realized her voluminous skirt would blow around while flying, so she made the practical decision to tie the skirt up tight around her ankles with cords.

Watching her forced to take tiny steps with her ankles bound, French fashion designer Paul Poiret was inspired both by her elegance and by the way the skirt hugged her figure, to create similar designs.

While the garment was lighter, compare to the heavy petticoat from the past, it was inconvenient and dangerous: women could only walk in very tiny steps, meaning they could barely lift their legs to get into cars or walk on staircases.

There was also no chance of running for their lives if there was an emergency. Some women tripped over their dress and drowned, or were trampled by horses simply because they were unable to run.

Along with many incidents involving tripping and falling, one of the terrifying deaths was reported in 1912 in the UK.

Ethel Lindley attempted to climb over a stile, but the skirt limited her movement and caused her to stumble. She broke her ankles, her bones stuck out from her flesh and she eventually died from septic poisoning.

Fortunately, the arrival of WWI meant the impractical nature of the hobble skirt was replaced – no longer could women afford the lack of mobility in a time of crisis and war.

Miniskirts are still banned in some countries today!?

London girls protesting for miniskirts during the 1960s.

The miniskirt has endured love, hate, and indifference through history.

First appearing in the 1950s and popularized by designer Mary Quant, the skimpy garment was initially deemed immodest and controversial – although many women wore it regardless, praising the flattering style for lengthening their legs.

In modern days, we might think the miniskirt is already accepted by society and no more than an ordinary item to wear. Surprisingly in some countries, miniskirt is still banned or controversial!

Take a look at what challenges miniskirts have faced, and are still facing, after all these years:

1960s
Banned in some European countries and deemed as an "invitation for rape" Coco Chanel and Christian Dior declared their distaste for the trend.

1970s
In South Korea, skirts start being measured by authorities, and if they were found too short women risked being fined or arrested.

Modern day
Multiple African countries, such as Uganda, continue to ban women from wearing miniskirts.

Did you know?
Mary Quant named the miniskirt after her favorite car – the Mini Cooper.

How did women go to the washroom with their "birdcage" dresses?

During the 18th century, ladies in large crinoline had special ways to take care of their bathroom business.

The large voluminous dresses of the 18th century were so impractical, they make one wonder how they got through doorways, let alone went to the bathroom.

Luckily, the birdcage-like crinoline under the dress was somewhat bendable, allowing women to sit down, and pass through doorways and small spaces. However, going to the toilet was still challenging with all the heavy petticoats and large crinolines to take care with.

An invention called the bourdaloue – or a "chamber pot" – was the solution, as it allowed a woman to go to the bathroom anywhere she pleased!

A lady would find a quiet corner, lift up the front of her crinoline, place the bourdaloue between her thighs and do her business standing up.

As these ladies who could afford such a large dress and crinoline would not be without a maid, she would then pass the bourdaloue to her maid to empty.

Keep in mind that in those days women didn't wear underwear and hygiene and privacy were not the priorities they are for us today, so while it may sound strange, back then, urinating in a pot wasn't considered weird at all!

Bourdaloue (1757–58)

FACTS ABOUT INTIMATE

The myth and facts of corset

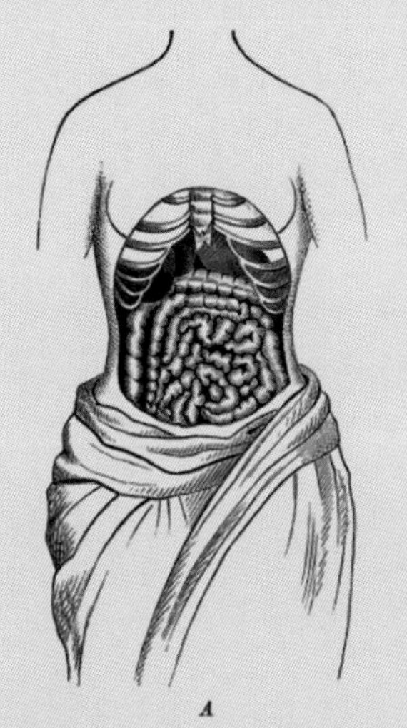

Intensities of a woman without corset

Intensities of a woman wearing a corset

The corset has been demonized as a torturing garment – cinching in a woman's waist and making breathing difficult. In reality, the garment has more history to it than just being a torture device.

Let's separate fact from fiction when it comes to the myths surrounding the corset.

<u>Only wealthy people wore corsets - FALSE</u>

Wearing a corset was something almost all women did as it was considered standard women's underwear, no matter rich or poor.

The only difference is, poor women wouldn't lace up their corsets as tightly as wealthy women.

Tiny 16-inch waists were the norm - FALSE

The extreme 16-inch waist-size – the result of wearing tightly bound corsets – was a trait of some wealthy women only.

Middle and lower class women often worked in labor-heavy jobs, so their priority was to be strong and healthy.

Wearing a corset might kill you -TRUE

A tightly laced corset restricts a person's ribcage and decreases lung capacity up to 30%. While the wearer would still be able to breathe normally without too much exertion, when doing vigorous activity in the corset, they could still suffocate and faint.

Lacing up a corset too tight can also cause muscle atrophy as well as other symptoms like indigestion, constipation and lower back pain.

If symptoms persist and the corset is not removed, it can even lead to death.

Wearing a corset is always incredibly painful - FALSE

The corset is undeniably uncomfortable, much like a bra, the corset was an undergarment women adjust to wear.

Girls started wearing corsets at an early age and are used to corsets. So, unless the wearer was suddenly trying to force herself into a much smaller size, the garment will feel restrictive but not painful.

French TV celebrity Jacques Angelvin shows the new inflatable push-up bra for the first time in France.

Watch out! Her bra is going to explode!

You may have heard the old wives tale of the inflatable bra that accidentally expanded and exploded on a plane. It turns out the urban legend is, in fact, a real-life incident involving an unsuspecting American woman named Betty Jenkins during the 1950s.

The inflatable bra helped women achieve their ideal cup size.

Containing a small plastic pouch that could be inflated with a mouthpiece, the bra expanded and contracted, allowing women to adjust their cup size daily.

But what seemed like a revolution for many women turned out to be an explosive invention – literally.

The story goes that Betty Jenkins blew her inflatable bra to her ideal cup size, 32, before boarding the plane to South America.

As the plane cabin was not pressurized, her bra quickly blew up to size 48 as the plane climbed to a certain attitude before exploding with a loud bang.

Luckily no one was injured, including Betty herself, but it caused chaos – the pop was so loud that the co-pilot emerged with a gun thinking there was a bomb.

The plane had to make an emergency landing, and Betty was handed over to the authorities to investigate whether she could be a terrorist. Betty was let go with a fine of $400 for the unscheduled delay.

The first sports bra was made by 2 jockstraps.

Jockstrap + Joke = Sports bra

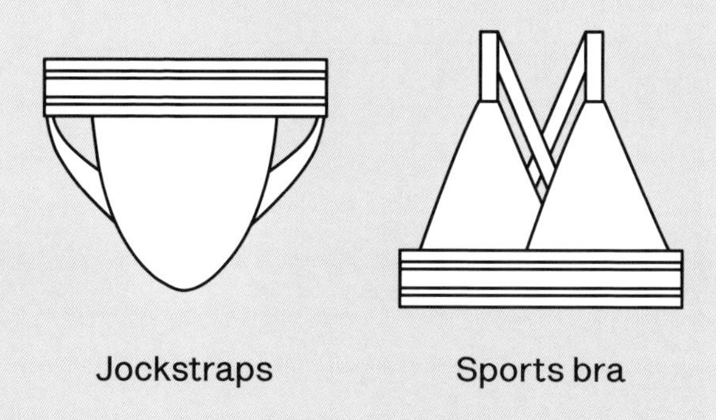

Jockstraps Sports bra

Did you know the sports bra started as a joke between a husband and wife?

Before sports bras were invented, women's options when it came to exercising were limited: wear no bra, wear a regular bra, or strap breasts down with tape. Clearly, none of these options were long term solutions for athletes or women who regularly exercised.

The idea for a sports bra clicked in 1977 when a woman called Lisa Lindahl took inspiration from her husband's joke – holding two jockstraps over his chest and suggesting that perhaps they could be a solution for her needs. Lisa did just that, and the first – albeit rather primitive – sports bra was born.

Men were the first to wear sexy garters?!

Today, garters usually refer to women's lingerie, but the first garter was worn by men and looked quite different.

The earliest men's garter was just a ribbon.

Did you know?
Still a tradition at many weddings today, the wedding garter is claimed to have originated in the dark ages. It was rumored that guests would join the bride and groom in the bedroom for good wishes and take a small item of the bride's clothing for luck – often the garter belt.

The garter band, an item of clothing used to hold up stockings, is often perceived as a sexy undergarment for women. But did you know it was men who wore them first?

As elastic was yet to be invented, garters were initially just ribbons that kept up the stockings of men from sliding down the leg.

Advanced versions began appearing in the 18th century featuring painful sounding buckles threaded with spiral swings to grip onto the legs.

Luckily, traditional elasticated socks eventually became popular, and men no longer needed garters.

So how did the garter belt transition from men's stockings support into sexy lingerie for women?

As women's hemlines rose in the 20th century, women began wearing the belt around the waist to keep their stockings up without having the garter belt exposed on the thigh.

It was then during the 1960s that women starting posing erotically wearing stockings and garter belts with slips, petticoats, and corsets.

Why did so many American women paint their legs during WW2?

Customers have their legs painted at a store in Croydon, London, so they can save their coupons which would otherwise be used for stockings.

Liquid stocking, made in Boston, Massachusetts., by the Langlois Company.

Today we can buy a pair of nylon or silk stocking easily, but guess what? During World War II, stockings were in such serious shortage that American and British women had to PAINT their legs to fake wearing a pair!

How did this come to be? The war was a time of strict limitations of many resources.

Silk and nylon was not just for making stockings, but also parachutes and naval gun bags. Therefore the government rationed these two materials, and encouraged women to donate their stockings to the army so they could be reused.

However, at that time, women who went out without stockings or hosiery were considered to not be properly dressed. So women got creative and invented their own liquid pairs called the liquid stocking.

They painted their legs with brown makeup paint, and sometimes even went as far as to draw on the "seam" of the stocking at the back of the legs with an eyebrow pencil – something that could easily go wrong without a steady hand. These "stockings" were reported to last up to three days if the wearer didn't have a bath!

The mayor of NYC ordered nude dancers to "put something on",
and that "something" was a G-string.

The man who made wearing a G-string in public "decent"

The G-string, or thong, may have been catapulted into popularity by someone you didn't expect – the mayor of New York City!

In 1939, then mayor Fiorello Henry La Guardia demanded that exotic dancers of New York wear something to cover themselves up while working, as the World's Fair was in town and he didn't want to jeopardize the reputation of the city.

Yet the dancers didn't want to lose business by covering up too much, so they chose the smallest solution they could find: underwear that could cover their private area while still showing their buttocks.

This marked the start of G-strings becoming a popular underwear choice for women.

Did you know?
The earliest ancestor of the thong dates back to ancient times. Worn by male tribe members in Africa, the garment was called a loincloth and was used to cover up the front groin area while leaving the buttocks bare.

The truth of the Guardian of Virginity

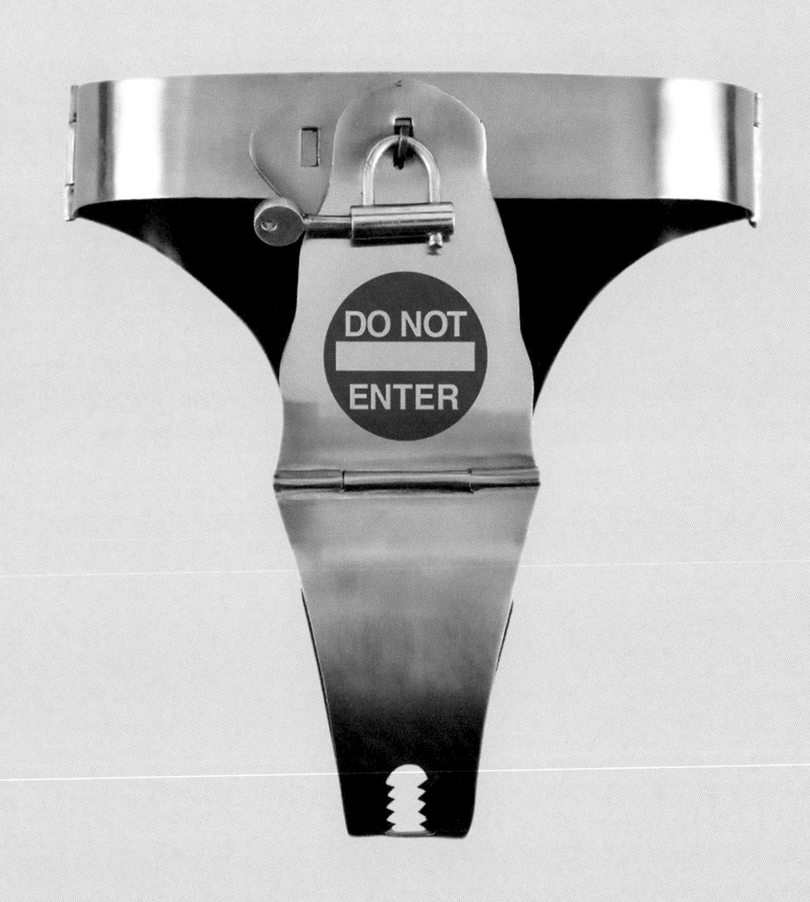

The chastity belt is often joked about when discussing being faithful in relationships, but is there any truth to the urban myth of the iron underpants?

It is rumored that during the age of the Crusades (between the 11th and 13th century) men would lock up their wives in iron underwear before they left the house to ensure they weren't tempted by other men.

The truth is, there is no real documentation to say if the chastity belt really existed at that time for such reasons, and a woman would not survive the consequent hygienic and health problems after several days of wearing a chastity belt.

There is one drawing of the belt reported in the 15th century. The sketch was sarcastic and alluded to the fact that ladies don't accept soldiers approaches "quite" so easily.

The documented uses for the chastity belt occurred later in history. In the Victorian era, it was used as a tool to stop women from masturbating, which was viewed as a health hazard at that time.

In the 19th century, some women wore them to work to protect themselves from sexual assault at their workplace.

Today, reports still exist of its use for different reasons. In one instance in 2016, a woman in Italy locked herself into a chastity belt to stop herself from getting into a sexual relationship. She had to call in the fire brigade to assist her when she lost the key!

Women holding lace underpants protesting against the ban of lace underwear in Almaty, Kazakhstan, on February 16, 2014.

Sorry ladies, no more lace underwear in Russia!

If you’re trying to find synthetic lace underwear in Russia, Belarus, and Kazakhstan, you won’t be in luck.

There is a regulation banning all underwear that contains less than 6% cotton from being sold, imported or produced in these countries. However, most of the lace underwear, especially from luxury brands, contain less than 4% cotton.

According to the government, the decision was made to protect the health of consumers against synthetic garments.

Why? Our body’s private areas are very sensitive, and synthetic fibers are not as breathable as cotton, trapping moisture that could cause bacteria, irritations and infections.

So, regardless of where you live, if you're needing some new underwear you might want to rethink those sexy, lacey pairs and opt for some simple cotton briefs instead!

Women wearing Turkish-style bloomer bathing suits made of flannel (1910).

Swimwear in the past, the heavier the better

Can you imagine wearing a swimsuit made of flannel? In the 19th century, this thick, non-revealing material was what was expected of women who chose to go to the beach.

Why?

Women's swimwear was not made for comfort or the ease of swimming. Instead, the primary purpose was to cover the skin and body shape as much as possible.

Showing your body in public was so immodest that some particularly vigilant women even rented a "bathing machine" – a contraption on wheels that could be dragged into the water, allowing a woman to jump in and out without being spotted.

The first woman to challenge the flannel swimsuit and wear something more form-fitting, revealing both her arms and legs, was Annette Kellermann.

Although Annette was arrested for indecent exposure at a public beach in Boston, she started a small movement – shifting the perception of how swimwear could look.

By 1910, the culture was changing, and although women still had to be modest, they were free to show their arms and the hemline length could be as high as mid-thigh.

However, go any higher than that and you might find yourself getting a fine from the "swimwear police" – who patrolled beaches and measured women's bathers! It wasn't until the 1930s that this rule diminished.

The bikini was named after the island Bikini Atoll, once used to test nuclear devices.

The mind “blowing” bikini

Everybody knows the bikini is a type of swimwear, but how many of us know that it was originally an island?

The island of Bikini Atoll was a testing site for nuclear devices in the 1940s and 1950s. Leading up to a notable test in 1946, Louis Réard was due to release his new creation – the sexy two-piece swimwear set.

Predicting the reaction to the swimwear would be as immediate and explosive as a nuclear bomb, he named the swimwear “bikini” too.

While the launch sent a few waves through the swimwear scene, it didn’t fully explode until the late 1950s, when Hollywood stars such as Betty Grable, Marilyn Monroe, Bridget Bardot and Esther Williams started wearing the swimwear style.

Even with its newfound approval amongst the masses, the lack of fabric and exposed flesh was still seen as scandalous, and the garment was banned in Spain, Belgium, Italy, the French Atlantic coastline, Portugal, Australia, and some American states after the first Miss World contest in 1951.

Did you know?
The creator of the bikini Louis Réard claimed the swimsuit could only be officially considered a bikini if it could be “pulled through a wedding ring.” This trick was to ensure it was small and revealing enough!

How does a Fastskin swimsuit makes you swim faster than you could be?

Speedo's Fastskin LZR Racer X Suit was inspired by shark's skin.

The notorious speed-breaking swimsuit "Fastskin LZR Racer" has been banned from many professional swimming competitions, including the Olympic Games and the FINA (Fédération Internationale de Natation).

Why?

The suit is deemed to give swimmers an unfair edge.

The ban took place after the 2008 Beijing Olympics, when the suit was said to turn the sport into a "technological arms race".

It was here that 25 new swimming world records were set, with only one of those record-breaking swimmers not wearing a Fastskin.

Adding to that, between 2000-2009, more than 100 swimming world records were broken while wearing the item – making it hard to believe the garment wasn't, at least in part, responsible.

So how does Fastskin technology work and why was it deemed so powerful?

The swimsuit was modeled after the tiny denticle-like surface sharks' skin, which creates a low-pressure zone that literally sucks the wearer forward.

Other features that may increase swimming performance include an extremely tight design, which helps to enhance a swimmer's posture, create a streamlined figure to reduce friction, and compress muscles to boost the wearer's circulation.

The Fastskin is actually so tight that it takes 30 minutes to put on, and has to be handled carefully in case the thin fabric tears.

Did you know?
The Fastskin is the creation of swimwear brand Speedo and is still available on the market today. However, the technology and the cost of the Fastskin makes it prohibitive to many – a single suit can cost upwards of $500 and can only be worn a handful of times before the technology loses its efficiency.

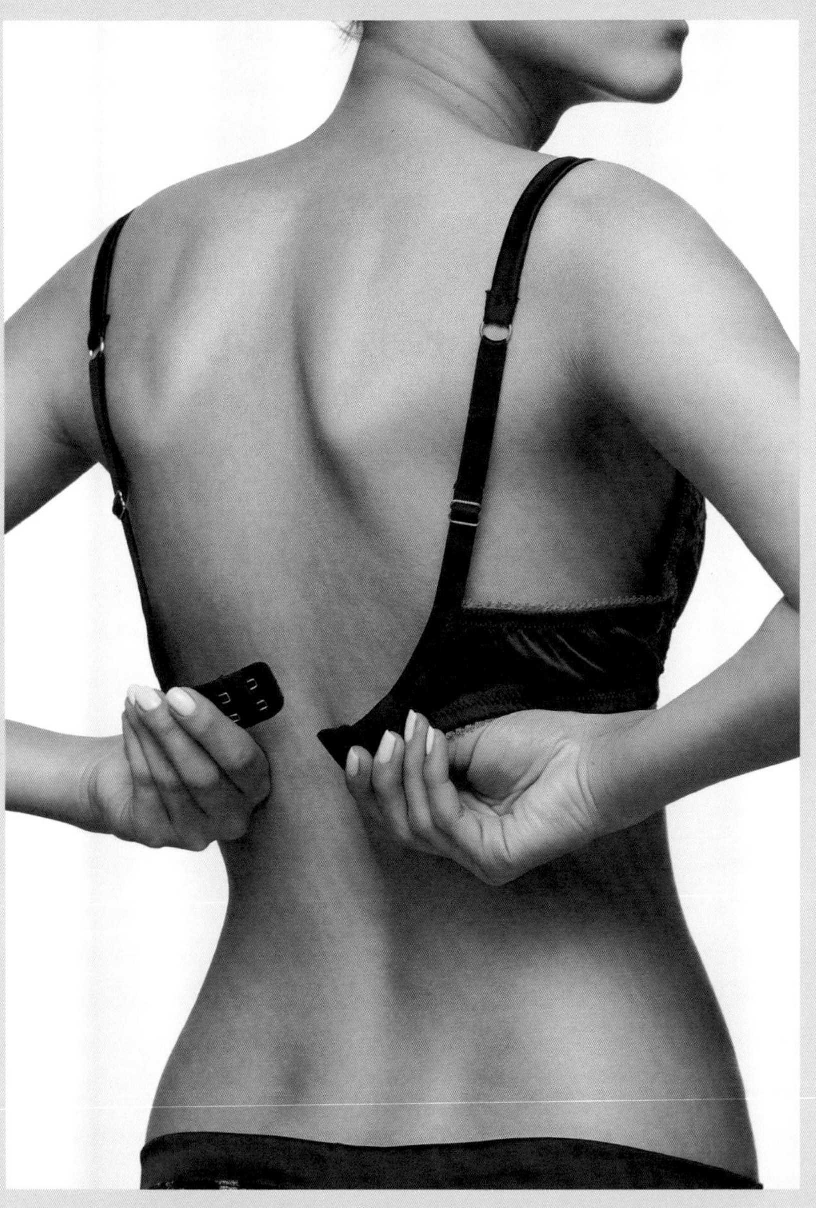

When trying on a new bra, always hook on the loosest back hook.

Don’t forget to do THIS when trying on a bra

Buying bras is notoriously difficult – with a whopping 80% of women said to be wearing the incorrect size in the United Kingdom. With so many of us getting it wrong, how do we start getting it right?

A bra should fit and support your breast comfortably. Generally speaking, slipping straps, gaping cup sizes and digging underwires are all indications that you might need a new bra, or professional help getting fitted.

It’s also very common for women to try on bras using the tightest back hook, but it is best to opt for a bra that fits on the loosest back hook instead.

Why?

Because with time and constant wear the bra elastic will slacken, which is when it’s time to start using the second and third hook.

Rotating bras through the week, and avoiding wearing the same bra too often, can slow down the stretching process of the undergarment and allow the garment to fit for longer.

FACTS ABOUT HACKS

Should I wash my jeans?

Levis's CEO Chip Bergh doesn't wash his jeans, why?

"A good pair of jeans doesn't really need to be washed in the washing machine except for very infrequently or rarely." - Chip Bergh, CEO of Levis Strauss & CO.

While most of our daily clothes are made to be washed after being worn a couple of times, denim is a surprising exception to the rule.

In fact, experts believe that frequent washing of denim jeans will cause the fabric to loosen and become misshapen.

It can also speed up fading – this is particularly the case for raw denim, as indigo only sets on the surface but doesn't penetrate the cotton fiber.

If your jeans are stained, do spot clean instead of washing the whole garment.

Of course if they start to smell you'll need to wash them – the presence of a bad odor is an indication of bacteria, which will break down the fabric.

According to denim experts, washing your jeans only when it is needed can extend the life span significantly.

But at the end of the day, it is a personal preference on how you care for your jeans, but the popular consensus seems to be: Do wash them but not too often and opt for spot cleaning to avoid unnecessary laundering. This will help you to prolong the life of your favorite pair.

Did you know?
The less you wash your raw denim jeans, the higher the contrast of the fade on the creases on key areas like the knees and groin.

Some clothes come with matching buttons and fabric – why?

A small piece of fabric might just save your garment

When we buy a shirt or jacket it's not uncommon to find spare buttons included – a handy extra when we inevitably lose a button and can't find an exact replacement.

What is less frequent – but is sometimes included with designer purchases or expensive clothing – is a piece of fabric that matches that of the garment.

While you might think it's for mending tears in the item, that piece of fabric is actually meant to be used as a wash test!

Washing this small square of fabric before your clothing can show you if the color bleeds, if the detergent damages the fabric, or if there are any other complications of washing such an expensive piece.

It's a thoughtful inclusion from brands to help consumers avoid damage, and prolong the longevity of the garment. So, next time you receive one, you know what to do!

Beware! Static electricity on clothes could cause an explosion

Beware! Static electricity could be dangerous.

If your job or workplace needs to be static electricity-free (such as electronic workers), you can always look for antistatic coveralls which are specially made for protection against electrostatic discharges.

It may sound dramatic, but the clothing you choose could help you avoid bursting into flames!

Static electricity – such as that shock you might feel when touching a metal doorknob while standing on a carpeted floor – is generally seen as harmless.

However, a report emerged of a firecracker worker in Hunan, China in 2018, who caused an explosion after accidentally igniting gunpowder from the static electricity on his clothing. While the man suffered injuries, luckily, he survived the incident.

These types of accidents are more likely to happen when you're surrounded by explosives or a large amount of fine powder at a high concentration, such as gas, gunpowder, flour and grains. Even a single spark of static electricity on your clothes could provoke an explosion while these powders are in the air.

So, what to do to minimize the risk of setting yourself on fire?

Choose natural fibers
Avoid synthetic fibers and choose cotton over wool.

Washing fabrics with a softener that coats the fibers and reduces friction can also help reduce the formation of static electricity.

Stay in a humid environment
Mist the air with a spray bottle or, even better, invest in a humidifier. Static charge isn't able to survive in humid air.

Rescue your favorite clothes from pilling!

It's so disappointing to get a new piece of clothing only to watch the fibers gather – or "pill" – into little fuzzy balls after the friction of regular wear.

To some extent it's inevitable, but short textures and synthetic materials exacerbate the problem – animal hair, acrylic, and Lycra being some of the worst culprits.

Just like the old saying "prevention is better than cure", the best way to avoid pilling is to understand the culprits, first.

How does pilling happen?

Short fiber + friction = fuzz ball
When fabrics rub together, the fiber ends start to break off and form small "fuzz balls".

Any ways to prevent pilling?

<u>Look for long-fiber material</u>
Long-staple cotton, silk or linen are less likely to pill than other animal hair and synthetic materials.

<u>Hand wash clothing</u>
The washing machine and the dryer cause friction, rubbing your clothes against each other. Instead, hand wash your garment as gently as possible and avoid pulling on the clothing.

<u>Turning clothes inside out before washing</u>
Pilling will happen on the inside of the garment while it's washed, meaning the result will be less noticeable.

<u>Use fabric softener</u>
This will coat the fibers, reducing the chances of fiber ends being rubbed off.

<u>Use a detergent containing enzymes</u>
The enzymes will help disintegrate the short fibers that cause pilling.

Bring Velcro back to life!

Velcro that no longer sticks can be so frustrating. As it ages, it not only looks cheap and unattractive but it can ruin your clothing, shoes or accessories. Plus, unlike buttons, Velcro isn't easy to replace.

Generally, when Velcro doesn't stick it's because of two issues that can be fixed: The hooks (the stiff side of the Velcro) are full of lint or dirt, or the loops (the fuzzy side of the Velcro) are frayed, causing the Velcro to not "stick" to the other side.

So, before you give up and toss those Velcro items in the bin, try a couple of these tricks to breathe new life into your belongings.

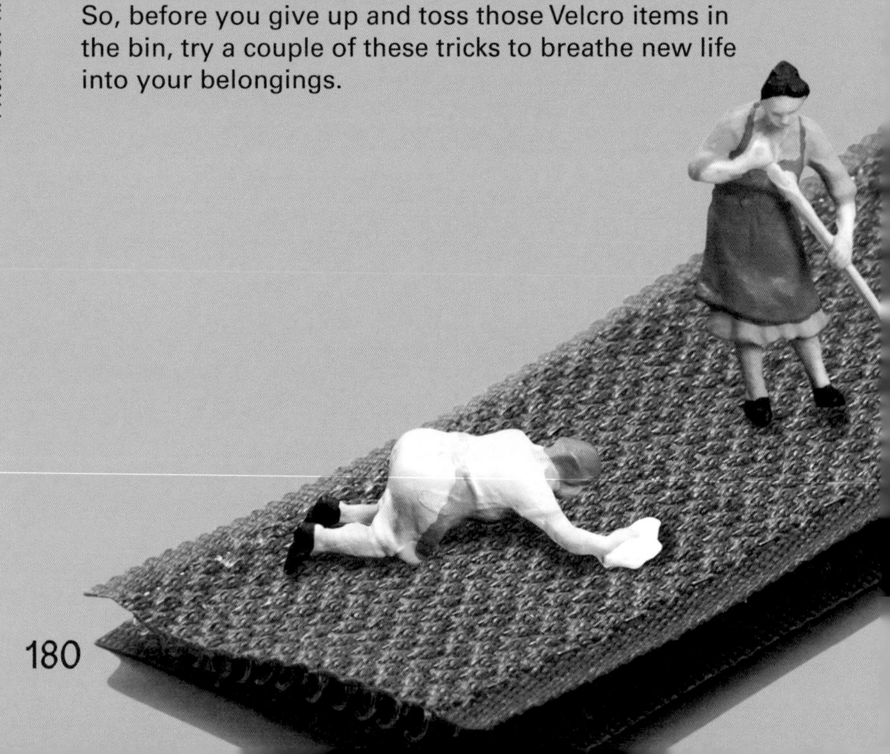

The hooks are full of lint or dirt

Brush Velcro with a toothbrush or a pet comb to remove the dirt. Once it's cleaned the hooks should grip the loops again.

The loops are frayed

Apply heat by using a lighter or a torch to make the loops or hooks curl again. Try to move quickly to avoid burning or melting the Velcro.

Dry cleaning isn't always the solution

What exactly is dry cleaning and why do we do it? It is a process which uses a chemical solvent instead of water so that materials that might get water-damaged (such as silk, rayon, cashmere or leather) can be cleaned safely.

While the gentle nature of dry cleaning is a major drawcard, it can be pricey if done regularly, and sometimes clothes that say 'dry clean only' on the tag might just need a simple hand-washing if they aren't stained too severely. You might even damage items more by dry cleaning them!

It can all get a little confusing, which is why we've broken down some recommendations to help you with the process.

What do you need to know before dry cleaning?

Downs and fabric containing plastic are best to not dry clean
Dry cleaning solvent might damage down jackets' filling, causing the filling to lose insulation, unless the care label indicates otherwise, or the dry cleaner is a specialist in down cleaning.

Meanwhile, material such as PVC or polyurethane can react poorly to dry cleaning agents and cause the material to peel or crack.

Some stains needs special treatment
Regular dry cleaning agents are good at removing grease and oil-based stains but not water-based stains or odors, such as sweat.

This is why it's important to tell the dry cleaner where and what kind of stain it is, as well as let them know if there are odors you want to get rid of. Then they can tailor the treatment specifically.

Not all stains can be cleaned
Keep in mind that there is no guarantee that your stains can be removed entirely or that the process won't damage your garment.

When the stains are too old and have been oxidized, the stains become very difficult, if not impossible, to remove.

Dry clean the whole set
If the item you need to dry clean is part of a set, take both to the dry cleaners. Your dry cleaner can inspect the color and sheen of the clean item and match it to the stained one during the process.

Once your garment is home from the dry cleaners, take it out of its plastic bag and let the clothes air out for at least a day before wearing it or storing it away, because there might be chemicals remaining in the garment.

DO NOT mix laundry detergent, fabric softener or sanitizer together!

Doing the laundry is not just about putting your dirty clothes and detergent into a washing machine and pressing the "start" button. There are many things you need to watch out for to ensure that garments are thoroughly cleaned and, most importantly, that they aren't ruined in the process.

The detergent and softener will neutralize each other

Fabric softener smooths the fabric by coating the fiber with a thin film of wax and oil, this might block the laundry detergent from penetrating the fiber to remove dirt and stains. Mixing detergent and sanitizer can set off a chemical reaction that weakens, or even neutralizes, the stain-removing and bacteria-killing effectiveness of both solutions.

Mixing detergent and sanitizer can also set off a chemical reaction that weakens, or even neutralizes effectiveness of both solutions.

If your washing machine has a dispenser draw with special compartments, simply follow the instructions and pour the solutions into the right place.

If you want to hand wash your clothes, rinse with laundry detergent or sanitizer, SEPARATELY, then rinse with fabric softener. Remember, fabric softener should always be used last.

Laundry detergent and sanitizer CANNOT replace each other

One misconception many people have is that either laundry detergent or sanitizer can get rid of BOTH dirt and bacteria. Remember, laundry detergent CANNOT kill germs, while sanitizer CANNOT get rid of dirt.

Did you know?
Pouring detergent, sanitizer or fabric softener directly onto clothes might stain and spot your clothes. The safest route is to pour the solution into the water and let it dissolve first, then put your clothes in.

Emergency first aid tips for your clothes

We've all been there. You spill something on your white skirt or pants when you don't have access to laundry detergent or stain remover.

So what do you do in an emergency situation when you need to be creative? We have some unconventional solutions including egg yolk, bread, and even beer.

Many household ingredients can be used to treat clothing stains.

Before applying any treatments, first, remove as much excess as possible:

For liquid stains, dab with a tissue, or more surprisingly, bread to soak up the surplus.

For solid or paste-based stains, make sure not to put pressure on it or rub the stain. Instead, use a business card or a butter knife to remove as much as possible.

Next, get to work by cleaning the stain with some of these rather handy "first aid" ingredients for different stains and rinse with water afterwards:

Oil-based pen ink
Rub with alcohol / hairspray / warm milk / tooth paste

Water-based pen ink
Soak with milk

Lipstick stain
Rub with rubbing alcohol / dish soap / nail polish remover or set still with hairspray

Red wine stain
Dab with vinegar and dish soap mixture / Flush with boiling water / white wine / vodka

Coffee stain
Soak with vinegar / dish soap / dab with egg yolk / blot with beer

Tea stain
Soak with vinegar

Oil stain
Dish soap / salt / baby powder / cornstarch

Ketchup stain
Rub with vinegar / dish soap

Blood stain
Rub with cola, or cold water mixed with salt / lemon juice / vinegar / cornstarch / aspirin powder / baking powder

Sweat stains and smell
Soak with vinegar / lemon juice / baking powder mixed with cold water

Smoke smell
Soak with vinegar / baking soda / lemon juice

Keep in mind that stains are always easier to deal with when they are fresh. It's also best not to iron garments before they are clean, as the heat could further set the stains into the fiber, making them more difficult to remove afterwards.

Website

acontinuouslean.com
allthatsinteresting.com
ancientpages.com
apetogentleman.com
artofmanliness.com
artsandculture.google.com
atlasobscura.com
attireclub.org
bbc.co.uk
bbc.com
bellatory.com
bespokeedge.com
blacklapel.com
bodyarmornews.com
bondsuits.com/
brandulation.com
business.time.com
businessinsider.com
businessinsider.com
scientificamerican.com
Buzzfeed.com
cbc.ca
cienciahistorica.com
cladwell.com
cleanipedia.com
completefrance.com
complex.com
contrado.co.uk
cosmeticsandskin.com
cottagelife.com
cup.com.hk
dailymail.co.uk
daks.com
designsponge.com
dictionary.com
eagleleather.com
edition.cnn.com
edwardianpromenade.com
etnet.com.hk
fashionencyclopedia.com
fashion-era.com
fashionisers.com
forbes.com
foxnews.com
garrisonbespoke.com
gentlemansgazette.com
gosfield-hall.co.uk
gq.com
grandeurtailors.com
greatist.com
groovyhistory.com
gulfnews.com
highsnobiety.com
huffingtonpost.com
hunker.com
ifuun.com
Independent.co.uk
insider.com
investopedia.com
io9.gizmodo.com
janeaustensworld.wordpress.com
japan-talk.com
josbank.com
journalofethics.ama-assn.org
kbtx.com
league91.com
lifebuzz.com
lifehacker.com
lovetoknow.com
lucafaloni.com
lucycorsetry.com
madamenoire.com
manmadediy.com
mashable.com
medium.com
menshealth.com
mentalfloss.com
menwit.com
mic.com
military1.com
news.harvard.edu
nydailynews.com
observer.com
parisiangentleman.co.uk
pictorial.jezebel.com
popbee.com
professionalelectric.biz
psychologytoday.com
quora.com
qz.com
racked.com
rd.com
read01.com
sarahsundin.com
saturdayeveningpost.com
sciencemag.org
scoopwhoop.com
skittishlibrary.co.uk
storm.sg
stylecaster.com
telegraph.co.uk
thealohashirt.com
theatlantic.com
thedailybeast.com
theenchantedmanor.com
thefactshop.com
thefashionlaw.com
thefittingroomonedward.com.au
thegartergirl.com
theguardian.com
theprivycounsel.blogspot.com
thespruce.com
thesun.co.uk
theuijunkie.com
thevintagenews.com
thirdlooks.com
thisisinsider.com
ties.com
time.com
townandcountrymag.com
vancouversun.com
vintagedancer.com
vogue.com.au
whowhatwear.com
wikihow.com
wikipedia.org
Woodywilson.com

Book

Credit Intelligence: Boosting Your Credit Smarts
Polly A. Bauer CPCS, Mava K. Heffler
BalboaPress

Fashion Victims : The Dangers of Dress Past and Present
Alison Matthews David
Bloomsbury Visual Arts

圖解日本裝束
池上良太
遠足文化事業股份有限公司

Image credits

16: Zun Zun / Pexels
18: Luke MacGregor / REUTERS
22: Arek Socha / Pixabay
22: Nathalie Lagneau / Catwalking / Getty Images
26: Shutterstock
28: Zentropa Entertainments / Photo 12 / Alamy Stock Photo
28: Allstar Picture Library / Alamy Stock Photo
32: Shutterstock
34: Museum of Selfies / Olivia Muss
40: Universal History Archive / UIG / Shutterstock
48: Shutterstock
50: Royal Collection Trust / © Her Majesty Queen Elizabeth II 2019
52: Gift of Woodman Thompson / The Metropolitan Museum of Art
54: Andrei Shupilo / Colourbox
64: Museum of Hartlepool / Hartlepool Borough Council
65: Morten Watkins / Solent News / Shutterstock
66: Courtesy Slawomir Lotysz / Ilustracja Polska, vol. 6, 1901
68: Theresa Moses (Illanaq), Yup'ik (Yupik Eskimo) / National Museum of the American Indian / Smithsonian Institution
72: Shutterstock
76: The 401st Bomb Group (H) Association
78-79: Toyo Enterprise
82: Shutterstock
94: Art Rickerby / The LIFE Picture Collection via Getty Images
100: George Grantham Bain Collection / US Library of Congress
112: Gianni Muratore / Alamy Stock Photo
120: Ng Han Guan / AP Photo
124: Photo 12 / Alamy Stock Photo
126: Nordiska museet
127: US Library of Congress
128: Granger - Historical Picture Archive
134: Gift of Woodman Thompson / The Metropolitan Museum of Art
136: Shutterstock
140: Larry Ellis / Express / Getty Images
142: Gift of Woodman Thompson / The Metropolitan Museum of Art
143: Bequest of R. Thornton Wilson, in memory of his wife, Florence Ellsworth Wilson, 1977 / The Metropolitan Museum of Art
146: Physiology for young people adapted to intermediate classes and common schools
148: Universal / Corbis / VCG via Getty Images
152-153: iStock
153: Bequest of William K. Vanderbilt, 1920 / The Metropolitan Museum of Art
154: G W Hales / Getty Images
155: Gift of Sidney Glaser / National Museum of American History / Smithsonian Institution
156: Shutterstock
160: Vladimir Tretyakov / AP Photo
166: iStock
168: Shutterstock
172: Shutterstock
176: iStock
184: Shutterstock

Acknowledgments

Chairman	Penter Yip
Editor in Chief	Sara Chow
Editor	Charlotte Chan
Art Direction & Design	Young & Innocent
Illustrator	Tong Chan
Photographer	Foo@rworkshop
Retoucher	Gabe Wong Lio Yeung
Copy Editor	Bridget Barnett
Proofread Editor	Nick O'Dell of HKNETS
Researchers	David Yiu Haylee Wong Rachel Fong Rosa Lo Yoyo Tsang

Contributors

We would like to thank all the contributors who gave us their sincere feedback and helped us make improvements to this project.

Hill Tse
Karmuel Young
Lau Kat Chun
Rainbow Lee
Ronnie Tung
Tammie Ho

Special thanks to Miss Arev Dinkjian and Mr Gerald Richards for their advice with language and editing.